Your Loved One
Lives On
Within You

Your Loved One Lives On Within You

Alexandra Kennedy

BERKLEY BOOKS, NEW YORK

YOUR LOVED ONE LIVES ON WITHIN YOU

A Berkley Book / published by arrangement with the author

PRINTING HISTORY
Berkley trade paperback edition / January 1997

The Putnam Berkley World Wide Web site address is
http://www.berkley.com/berkley

ISBN: 0-425-15453-X

BERKLEY®
Berkley Books are published by
The Berkley Publishing Group,
200 Madison Avenue, New York, New York 10016.
BERKLEY and the "B" design
are trademarks belonging to Berkley Publishing Corporation.

PRINTED IN THE UNITED STATES OF AMERICA

10 9 8 7 6 5 4 3 2 1

For Jon

Acknowledgments

I especially want to acknowledge my editor at Berkley, Hillary Cige, for her enthusiastic support of this book; Suzanne Lipsett whose expert feedback and careful editing enormously improved it; my agent, Laurie Fox, for her deep commitment to excellence and the pleasure of working with her; and Kathryn Hall, for promoting my work with such grace and perseverance. The team at Berkley deserves much appreciation for the care and attention they gave to birth this book.

My profound thanks to my students at the Institute of Transpersonal Psychology whose contributions have greatly enriched this book, to my clients who inspire me with their courage in the face of grief, and to all those who shared their stories in workshops, letters and interviews. To honor confidentiality, I have changed names and identifying details, except when requested to do otherwise.

To my friends who offered their love, moral support and fresh ideas—thank you! I wish I had space here to name you all but I hold every one of you in my heart in gratitude. My thanks also to Ken Ring, Michael Toms and Hal Bennett for their wise words and encouragement and to Robert Frager for bringing me into the ITP family three years ago. To Patty Flowers at University of California Santa Cruz Extension, I offer my loving gratitude for her friendship and belief in me—and for offering my first class on this subject. Ned Hearn, Rob Sals and Matthew Berger have been generous with their counsel.

I feel grateful beyond measure to my family for their enduring love and generosity, especially my mother, Dan, Van and Beth, Bob and Dawn—as well as my father who has been such a nurturing presence within me. My son deserves special thanks for his contribution of hugs, passionate drumming, and adolescent perspective. I am truly blessed that this heartful and talented young man is my son. My husband, Jon, once again has been my toughest critic and greatest support. His love, intelligence, and guidance permeate this book and every aspect of my life. After twenty-five years of marriage he is—more than ever—the love of my life. This book is dedicated to him.

Contents

❧

Introduction

Very few of us ever fully express our love for another. Afraid of being hurt, we find ourselves unwilling to be as vulnerable and open as that admission requires. Despite our efforts to avoid hurts and resentments, however, they inevitably build up in our relationships with family and friends. Unaired, such hurts close our hearts and create distance between ourselves and our loved ones, further increasing the difficulty of expressing our love and appreciation. So, when a loved one dies, we may find ourselves filled with regret for all that remained unspoken. The realization that all opportunities have passed for that last talk, or even just a good-bye, can be agonizing. Many of my clients have said, about a mother, grandmother, or sister, "How I wish I had told her I loved her before she died." This kind of unfinished business can prevent us from letting go and moving on with our lives. In our grief, our old resentments, regrets, and unexpressed love can gnaw at us, creating wounds that contaminate all our other relationships.

You may consider it impossible to turn around such unresolved issues, resigning yourself to living with your memories, regrets, and disappointments. It is true that you will never again be in the physical presence of the loved one who has died, and I in no way mean to diminish the excruciating pain of coming to terms with the finality of death. Years after my father's death, I still ache for the touch of his warm hand on mine and long to hear his voice or see him just one more time.

Yet I rejoice in the times when my father appears to me in my dreams and meditations. His body is strong and vital and he holds his chest and shoulders proudly, just as he did in his life. His hair is lightly streaked with gray, his brown eyes soft and accessible. In these moments, I can reach out and feel the warmth of his hand and hear his voice, filling the space with a comforting resonance. My heart knows that death did not erase our relationship. On the contrary, in the dark shadow of grief, my relationship with my father has grown in sweetness.

It was during his illness that I made the discovery that I could inwardly connect with my father. I vividly remember the day he was diagnosed, a bleak one even though the sun was shining. It seemed to me that the colors had drained out of the earth and sky. I felt overwhelmed and desperate. The cancer had already metastasized throughout his bones.

Despite the fact that recovery seemed very unlikely, my father went on with his life as though nothing had happened, keeping the diagnosis secret from his friends and business associates. Each day, he went off to work as usual; each night, he collapsed in pain. He refused to talk about dying with me or my mother. I wanted to break down with him, share my terror of losing him.

After crying for hours one day, I collapsed in front of a black and white photograph of my father. He was sitting nobly with his chair tipped back, wearing a crisp white shirt with the sleeves rolled up, his tie pulled to one side, a generous smile across his face. Looking at the image, I realized that my dad was going to die as he had lived: with denial, dignity, and courage.

Closing my eyes, I prayed for help in facing the loss of my father. For a long time, I sat with my pain in silence.

There was no answer, no insight, just empty space and the sensation of hot pain in my chest. Suddenly a dolphin surged to the surface of my mind. It was followed by others, all weaving golden threads around the Earth. Even though it made no sense, this spontaneous image lightened my heart. I hoped it was a response to my prayer, but it still wasn't clear how it could be.

The next day I sat again in silence, opening myself to whatever might happen. This time, when I closed my eyes, I saw an image of my father slumped in a chair while an unknown woman cared tenderly for him. Absorbed in his pain, he was silent, but I knew he was aware of and grateful for my presence. I realized, too, that my father lived within me as vividly as he did in my outer life. From that time on, our inner relationship unfolded in both dreams and meditations. He held me as I cried; I held him as he shook with pain. We talked about past hurts and resentments. He was vulnerable and open with me in a way that he had not been before. Our relationship grew stronger throughout his short illness, and his death transformed him—within me, he became wiser, freer, more loving, and more expressive. Our relationship grew sweeter and closer.

To the imagination, death is not an ending, not a catastrophe, but a transformation. Within you, your loved one lives on and, with your participation, your mutual relationship will grow and change. In this book, I will help you reach this special relationship through your imagination, using practical, effective methods to resolve old hurts; share your appreciations and disappointments; express your sometimes pure, sometimes ambivalent, love; and update your relationships by integrating the changes and new insights that have occurred to you since your loved one's death.

As you work with the exercises in this book, try to set aside your assumptions and expectations. Note especially as we proceed that it is important to keep old images and memories from dictating the nature of the relationship after death. Be open to new possibilities. You have the power within yourself to create and re-create your relationships, to heal old wounds, to experience deep intimacy. Reconnect with your beloved, restore the lost dialogue, transform an absence into a presence. All that is keeping you from a sense of connection with your loved one is your unused imagination.

It is my hope that you will use the techniques in this book to restore communication and open your heart to a transformed relationship. Death is an ending, but it is also a beginning. The future is still open. Your lost beloved is within reach—within *you*—much closer than you think.

PART 1

Looking Within

The presence of that absence is everywhere.

EDNA ST. VINCENT MILLAY

Chapter 1

The Living Presence Within You

When a loved one dies, many people are filled with regret for all that was never expressed between them. It can be agonizing to realize that all opportunities are gone for that last talk, the chance to say the unsaid, and tie up loose ends. With old hurts unhealed, good-byes unspoken, or love unexpressed, this situation can result in frustration, guilt, bitterness, obsessive thinking—even an inability to go on with one's life.

In their regret, people often go over and over their last encounter with a loved one, focusing with excruciating detail on what was and was not said. Again and again clients tell me,

- "How I wish I had told him I loved him before he died."
- "I wish I hadn't said so many hurtful things that day. I didn't know it would be our last talk."
- "I was in such a hurry. It was one of the few days when I stayed only for a little while, and we hardly spoke at all."

So many regrets: that one hadn't been present at the moment of death; that there had been no chance to say good-bye; that so many chances for meaningful interaction had been

3

overlooked; even for all the times long before the dying when one had forgotten to call or write or had put off doing so. But in my experience, the deepest regret—and the one with the sharpest sting—attends the failure to say, "I love you." This seems to be the most important message we can communicate to each other, and too often we feel there's so much time to express our love that we simply put off doing so.

Marta came to one of my Losing a Parent workshops, where she shared with the group that in grieving the death of her father, she was consumed with regret and self-blame. Dismayed by her father's alcoholism and abusive conduct, she had cut off contact with him months before he died. She felt that by distancing herself from her father, she would develop healthier ways of relating to him once she resumed contact. Then late one night, after several months of silence, her father phoned her, sounding desperate. He was drunk, his words slurred. Wanting no part of the conversation, she told him she would talk to him when he was sober and hung up the phone. The next morning, the police called Marta to inform her that her father had been found dead in his apartment. She was devastated. Months later, she still felt so overwhelmed by regret and guilt that she was having difficulty functioning in her daily life. "If only I had gone to his house that night," she told us, "he might still be alive today. I feel so terrible and ashamed that the months I pulled away from him were the last months of his life." Marta's situation is dramatic, but others, less clear-cut, can still be intensely painful. To assess the quality of your feelings surrounding the closure of a loved one's death, ask yourself:

- Did I express my love? Did I share my appreciations?
- Were we able to be open and honest with one another?
- What were the issues in our relationship that we did not talk about?
- Were there conflicts between us that remained unresolved at the death?

- Do I feel any regrets?
- Do I still harbor resentments from the past?
- Was anything left unsaid?
- Did I say good-bye?

Perhaps you are hoping that your grief will take care of itself and that your regrets will dissolve in time. Perhaps you feel that it's too late: "She's dead. What's the use?" Such hopes, as clinical practice and research show, are usually disappointed. Unresolved grief—regrets and disappointments that remain unacknowledged and unaddressed—continues to work silently and insidiously within the person left behind, resulting in such symptoms as apathy, social isolation, addiction, chronic physical problems, fearfulness, depression, overworking, and compulsive behavior. The antidote to these symptoms is to look, open-eyed, at the leave-taking once more in order to identify and resolve unaddressed issues.

In this chapter, I introduce two concepts that can change your perception of loss forever: your loved one lives on within you, and you can gain access to this relationship through your imagination. I also introduce a powerful method based on these principles that will enable you to communicate *internally* with your deceased loved one and resolve unfinished business, express your love, and feel more at peace with yourself. In later chapters, we'll be concerned with technique—how, in practical terms, to put these principles to work. For now, however, in this introductory chapter, my goal is to reassure you that the tools do indeed exist for reconnecting with the person you may have considered lost forever.

JUST BEHIND THE DOOR

Most of us see death as an ending, a final loss. We assume that a door has closed, our loved one has gone, and gone, too, are any possibilities for reconciliation. It is true that the old relationship has come to an end. You will never again be in the physical presence of the person. However, death need not cut you off from those you love. An inner relationship with the person who has died continues on after death. This relationship, constantly unfolding within, offers powerful and mostly untapped opportunities for healing, resolution, and even guidance. It is said that every ending brings a new beginning. So it is that the end of a life can bring a new beginning in your relationship with the person you consider lost to you forever.

For many, this concept is new and hard to accept. You may resist the idea at first, but if you're willing to experiment with the methods presented in this book, you will experience this inner relationship directly. Once that happens, you will never again doubt that your beloved lives on—within you.

You may have already had a dream or dreams about the person, dreams that seemed so real that you have awakened wondering whether he or she were still alive after all. Dreams often give us first glimpses of this ongoing relationship. Psychologist Carl Jung had this reaction when he dreamed about his deceased father six weeks after the elder's death: "Suddenly he stood before me and said that he was coming back from his holiday. He had made a good recovery and was now coming home. I thought he would be annoyed with me for having moved into his room. But not a bit of it! Nevertheless, I felt ashamed because I had imagined he was dead. . . . Later I kept asking myself: 'What does it mean that my father returns in dreams and that he seems so real?' It was an unforgettable experience, and it forced me for the first time to think about life after death" (Jung, p. 96).

In an example closer to home, the night after his death, the husband of Brenda, a workshop participant, appeared to her in a dream. When Brenda expressed surprise that her husband stood before her, radiant and healthy, he gently admonished her, "I never left you." Many such dreams share a common theme: the deceased takes for granted that the relationship is ongoing, while the griever/dreamer struggles to accept this new concept.

How common are these dreams? Numerous studies have focused on after-death contacts. In 1984, the National Opinion Research Council conducted a general public survey of contact experiences with the dead. Sixty-seven percent of people with deceased spouses reported such contacts, while 42 percent of the general public makes such claims. In 1976, researchers Kalish and Reynolds wrote about after-death contacts in their book *Death and Ethnicity*. Based on their research, 50 percent of women and 30 percent of men reported this contact, and the most commonly reported form was through dreams.

I, myself, cannot be sure if these experiences involve actual contact with the dead—no one can—but the very existence of these contact experiences attests to the fact that our loved ones live on in us in the form of an inner presence. Rather than debate the reality of these experiences, let us focus on those indisputable inner relationships with our deceased loved ones, developing them, deepening them, and learning to enjoy them. The door into these places of contact is the imagination, as the story of Rita, another participant in one of my workshops, dramatically illustrates. Through your imagination you can experience this relationship for yourself, as Rita did in a grief workshop that I led. I had guided Rita to enter an imaginary house where she would meet her husband.

RITA'S STORY

As Rita stepped over the threshold into the living room, she marveled at the vision of her husband. Dressed in a faded blue T-shirt, khakis, and grass-stained tennis shoes, he sat in a burgundy armchair, his chin resting comfortably on one hand. Shaken by the suddenness of the encounter, Rita paused and looked at Barry more carefully; it had been months since she had last seen him. The expression in his brown eyes was both loving and playful. The small worry lines across his forehead had disappeared, as had the tension in his jaw. Once driven and intense, Barry now sat tranquilly, as though he had all the time in the world.

Her heart thumping wildly in her chest, Rita approached him. She had assumed that she would never again hold him or talk to him. She had struggled to grieve without saying good-bye, without telling him how much she loved him. And yet here he was in her imagination—and the experience was so real. As they embraced, she could feel the warmth of his body.

Rita spoke first, asking the questions that had kept her awake night after night. "Barry, what happened to you? Were you lonely as you lay dying? Were you frightened? Did you think of me?" The familiar sound of his voice both startled and consoled Rita. "It all happened so quickly. One moment I was standing at the airline counter; the next I was overcome with a stabbing pain in my chest. I couldn't breathe. I did feel frightened, but only briefly. Then everything went black."

Rita reflected for a few minutes, feeling a sense of relief that he hadn't suffered long. Then it hit her that he hadn't thought about her at all before he died. She felt angry, and then ashamed for being so selfish. Already she was struggling with the same conflicts and insecurities she had experienced throughout their relationship. "I thought you would never die. I thought I had plenty of time to tell you how much I adored you. I was scared to admit even to myself how much you meant to me. I wanted to feel safe first, so you could reassure me that you loved me more than your work. I regret that I focused so much on my own protection and so little on our connection. I miss you terribly."

"Rita," Barry responded, "I need you to know that I never cared more about my work than I cared for you, even though it may have appeared that way. It was easier for me

to lose myself in my work because it made me feel successful. At home, I often felt defeated and unappreciated. You
were frustrated with me so much of the time and you let me
know it! I didn't talk enough, I didn't help out enough, I
didn't understand you. If I had our marriage to do over
again, I would support and cherish you more. I would listen
to you more. You must realize that I am no longer who I
was in your life. We can't share the special moments of our
daily lives together anymore. But I never left you. I'm here,
full of love for you."

Stroking her husband's hair, Rita spoke softly. "Why
couldn't we have talked like this when you were alive! And
yet I can't imagine sharing these things with you before. So
many times since you died I've called out desperately to you,
'Talk to me!' And there was no answer. I've felt angry that
you deserted me and guilty that I wasn't there when you
died. Now I just want to feel close to you. Will you hold me
awhile, Barry?"

Barry held Rita in his arms. At first she wept; then, in
silence and stillness, their souls embraced. As they finally
drew apart, Rita whispered in the ear of her beloved, "I
know now that you live on in my heart. I love you so much!
And I'm not afraid to feel it."

"I love you, Rita." And they both laughed.

IMAGINATION: THE BRIDGE

In making contact as Rita did with Barry, imagination is the
bridge, connecting our external reality and the internal world
of our psyche. With our loved ones present within us, imagination renders death not an ending but a transformation.

Many other cultures have turned to the imagination as a
valuable resource for grieving. In *Imagery in Healing*, author
Dr. Jeanne Achterberg calls the imagination our "oldest and
greatest healing resource" (Achterberg, p. 3). For thousands

of years, shamans throughout the world have traveled in a
trance state into invisible worlds to consult with the spirits
of the deceased and serving as messengers between the
worlds. The *Tibetan Book of the Dead* provides texts for the
living to read to the deceased that describe what to expect,
what to avoid, and what to look for in the transitional states
after death. The Confucian and Buddhist religions teach that
each household should have an altar that is dedicated to the
family ancestors. Daily observance at this altar facilitates ongoing contact with the deceased. The living family members
converse with the photographs set on the altar and place gifts
there for the dead. In exchange, the ancestors are expected
to maintain a living presence in the house, providing guidance and inspiration. In the Middle Ages, the common practice of holding conversations with the souls of the departed
provided comfort and reassurance to those who were grieving. The Swiss-German physician and alchemist Paracelsus
wrote, "Everyone can educate and regulate his imagination
so as to come thereby into contact with spirits, and be taught
by them." (Walsh, p. 119) In contemporary Australia, Aborigines continue the ancient practice of talking to the spirits,
which emerge from rocks that have been rubbed together
for three days. The Aborigines believe that their dead ancestors return to share both mythic and practical information. In many cultures, then, death is no barrier to
communication because they have actively utilized the imagination when faced with this inevitable transition.

Many myths remind us that our relationship with a beloved can be restored, even when death has occurred. Think
of the Egyptian goddess Isis and her husband/brother Osiris.
Osiris, having been killed by conspirators, is locked in a coffin and sent down the Nile. In a state of deep grief, Isis
searches for and finally finds her husband's body. However,
while she is visiting with her son, one of the conspirators
cuts up the body and scatters the pieces. With the help of
the gods, Isis pieces the body together and Osiris comes back

to life. He then reigns as king of the dead in the Underworld. The Greek myth of Demeter and Persephone presents a similar theme. When Persephone is abducted into the Underworld by the god of death, her mother, Demeter, is devastated with grief, and refuses to allow any vegetation to grow on Earth. She bargains with the gods of Olympus for her daughter's return, and, with the help of the messenger god, Persephone and Demeter are reunited. However, since Persephone has eaten three pomegranate seeds before leaving Hades, she must spend three months a year in the Underworld, where she reigns as queen.

Most ancient cultures have myths conveying the interwoven themes of loss, search, and recovery, as though to remind people that it is possible to reconnect with deceased loved ones. But in our modern world, which values technology over tribal practices, the power and even the existence of invisible worlds has been denied. Imagination has been relegated to fantasy and at times considered abnormal. "Oh, it's just your imagination," people tell us condescendingly. And so, our most valuable resource in the grieving process has been devalued and all but lost to us.

The methods described in this book are designed to help nurture your power of imagination. You may argue that you just aren't an imaginative person, but be assured that imagination is a natural and universal faculty. Everyone has it, though in many it remains muted and undeveloped.

Many authors and practitioners in many different fields, including modern medicine and psychology, have researched, written about, and used imagination in their work with clients. All have come to a similar conclusion: that imagination has been an important resource for healing since the beginning of history, and it is time for our culture to acknowledge its usefulness for healing both body and psyche. All the techniques you'll learn in subsequent chapters are tied to the use of imagination in nurturing and deepening your inner communication.

FOSTERING YOUR IMAGINATION

Although imagination is part of our psychic birthright, many people have let this powerful faculty go dormant. However, certain psychological states such as grief and depression seem to activate the imagination naturally. People who are grieving find that they have little energy or enthusiasm for external reality; their energy is drawn inward. As grief dampens their outer senses, it can open inner senses, giving them new acuity in seeing, hearing, and feeling what is inaccessible to our senses during normal times. After her husband's death, the world looked dull and flat to Rita. However, when she slept, her dreams burst with vivid imagery and vibrant colors. In a workshop setting, she followed my instructions to take her time to fully experience the sights, sounds, and smells of an imaginary house. She readily made the transition to an inner world where she had a profoundly moving encounter with her husband. Experiencing this inner world directly through her senses definitely fostered her imagination.

Psychologist Jean Houston affirms that wounding can open the doors of our sensibility to a larger reality, one that we usually fail to perceive. In my grief workshops, I have been struck with the ease and openness with which participants are able to work with exercises involving the imagination—even participants who have long considered themselves not to be highly imaginative. People who rarely remember their dreams may report vivid dreams when they are grieving.

Although grief may jump-start the inner senses, most people who do not regularly use the imagination find that it takes concentration and energy to fully awaken these atrophied senses. If you have ever had to work on atrophied muscles after weeks of disuse, you know what effort is required. The same is true when you begin to work on activating the inner senses:

you may get discouraged because you can't "see" anything. In this context, it is unfortunate that such activation is often associated with the visualization of imagery. Not everyone visualizes; in fact, about 40 percent do not. Many people do experience imagery through hearing, touch, or movement, but others just "sense things." Even if you can visualize, "seeing into the other world requires a different kind of seeing that we have almost, it seems, forgotten how to do" (Larsen, p. xix). While one sense may naturally be stronger, I encourage you to work on activating all your inner senses. The following exercise will help you do this. Remember that the important step of awakening your inner senses will facilitate the flow and vividness of your imagination.

EXERCISE 1

Awakening Your Inner Senses

Close your eyes. Let your attention first focus on your breathing. Be aware of the sensations you experience with every inhalation and exhalation. Now, imagine yourself standing in the center of a kitchen. There is an open fireplace in one corner. You can hear the crackling of the fire. Move closer and hold up your hands to the fire. Feel the heat. Look closely at the colors in the flames. On an iron stand in the fireplace a pot is simmering, soup bubbling over. Smell the aromas. Focus on this, seeing if you can identify what is cooking. You might even be able to smell herbs flavoring the soup. There is a wooden spoon sitting next to the pot. Pick it up, feeling its texture and weight. Dip it into the pot of soup and scoop out some to taste. Savor it in your mouth, feeling your taste buds responding.

In the imagination, we are not limited to the laws of ordinary reality. There we can fly, we can change form, we can do things that would be impossible in daily life. It takes a while to adjust and open fully to these freedoms, freedoms that enable us to experience relationships from new perspectives. Be willing to let go of your expectations regarding the limitations of daily life. Consider the wonderful benefits of crossing the border of the possible in the story of Susan, a client.

Susan had been frightened of her domineering father ever since she was a little girl. Even as an adult, she avoided talking to him about anything that might provoke his wrath. After her father's death, she felt angry at herself for her lack of courage and for her passivity in her relationship with him. She never felt free of him, only haunted by all that had been left unsaid. In a therapy session, she decided to work with her imagination in order finally to confront her father. Closing her eyes, she saw him in his red plaid shirt, standing before her. Being a tall man, he towered over her, and she felt as small and vulnerable as she had as a child. A familiar feeling of paralysis overtook her, and she was unable to speak. Suddenly, she discovered that she was slowly rising up off the floor, levitating until she was looking down on her father. From this new perspective, Susan felt safer, stronger, and clearer. She voiced all the feelings, resentments, and longings she had held back from him. As she talked, she noticed something stirring in her chest that she had never felt in her father's presence before: tenderness. If she had interrupted the flow of imagination by saying, "But I can't levitate! I can't fly!" she would not have had this experience of healing.

It is important to approach the imagination with a non-judgmental, nonanalytical, receptive awareness. So many times my clients will judge or edit what is happening as they explore the imagination. They try to change an image because they don't understand or don't like it. This interference inhibits the richness, wisdom, and mystery of the imagination.

Last but not least, approach the imagination with respect. This faculty is enormously powerful. In 1942, during World War II, Carl Jung gave a lecture on "Der Geist Mercurius" (the Spirit Mercury), in which he warned that imagination could either be a force of healing or of destruction. To illustrate, he told a story from the brothers Grimm called "The Spirit in the Bottle," which I paraphrase here.

A young man was so poor that he was unable to complete his education. One day, he found a bottle, from which a voice cried out, "Let me out!" The man opened the bottle and a mighty spirit rose up, as big as the oak tree under which the bottle had lain. "I am the powerful Mercury," boomed the spirit. "I was shut up in this bottle as penance. Whoever lets me loose, I will break his neck." The young man realized that his only hope in saving his life was to entice the spirit back into the bottle. "I cannot believe that such a mighty spirit could come out of such a little bottle," he told the spirit with awe. "Could you show me how you did that?" The spirit immediately obliged, and the young man rammed the stopper back into the bottle. With that, the situation had changed: Mercury was contained; but this time, the young man was aware of his power. The spirit begged the young man to free him again, but now Mercury offered a reward in exchange for his freedom: a cloth that would turn anything it rubbed into silver. Pleased with this exchange, the young man set the spirit free. Using the cloth to create silver, he made enough money to complete his studies and became a famous doctor.

This story demonstrates the need to approach Mercury, the spirit of imagination, with great respect. Otherwise, he can become destructive. At first, the young man does not know of Mercury's great powers, so when he releases the spirit, he endangers himself. To save himself from destruction, he must find a way to contain the power. Only then can he begin to work with Mercury to his benefit. To do that, he must communicate with Mercury and work out a mutually satisfactory relationship. That done, he can dare to let the power out of the bottle again, this time in the service of healing, using Mercury's powers to become a doctor. The young man is now richer than he was—and wiser. In order to use the gift of imagination to help you heal your relationships, you must be humble in its presence and respectful of its power.

COMMON PROBLEMS

Some people have difficulty working with the imagination, especially in the beginning. If this is true for you, it will help you to know that you will go through three different stages as you develop your capacity to work with the imagination. In the first stage, many people struggle, unable to imagine, see, hear, touch, or sense anything out of the ordinary. In this stage, simply remind yourself that imagination is a natural faculty, that everyone has it, and that it is accessible within you. If you work toward activating your inner senses persistently and patiently, they will gradually strengthen. You may not be able to see actual images that are inaccessible in the ordinary world, but you may be able to sense or even hear things. Pay careful attention to everything that happens, no matter how subtle or insignificant.

In the second stage, you will begin to experience imagery, but you may question it and ask yourself, *Am I making this up? Is this real?* Realize that this questioning, which often interrupts the flow of imagery, is a completely normal response. Notice that you are doubting your experience, but don't let your doubts stop you from exploring. Remember: this is just a stage, one that most people pass through as their imagination continues to develop.

In the third stage, images will begin to occur spontaneously and uninhibitedly. Now, you may realize that the world you are exploring in the imagination is as real as anything you have experienced in ordinary reality. Jungian analyst Mary Watkins expressed this succinctly: "Going into the imaginal then becomes not a matter of preserving oneself in a foreign land but rather of returning home" (Watkins, p. 118).

Be patient and thorough as you develop imagination skills. You are preparing to meet and interact with a deceased loved one. Imagination will enable you to walk across the silent chasm of death and touch, see, and talk with this person.

THE NEED FOR DIALOGUE

Psychologist Louise Kaplan asserts in her book, *No Voice Is Ever Wholly Lost*, that "dialogue is the heartbeat of human existence . . . we cannot live without it" (Kaplan, p. 239). She sees this factor as playing such a pivotal role in our lives that we dread the loss of it more than actual extinction.

Much has been written in the field of developmental psychology that confirms the critical importance of dialogue, even in the earliest days of infancy. In this context, it's easy to understand how the cessation of dialogue when a loved one dies can be devastating. "We cripple our own selves and even destroy the world around us in our desperate quest to refind, recover, restore, reconstitute a lost dialogue" (Kaplan, p. 239). When our efforts to reconnect fail, we may feel helpless to resolve unfinished business and unable to reach peace with our loss.

Many people secretly or unconsciously attempt to carry on a lost dialogue with a loved one. For example, a person might talk to a deceased spouse over morning coffee. A grieving mother may converse with her deceased child while sorting through his toys or clothes. Often, people keep these communications secret for fear of being misunderstood by the living. They hold these conversations without any understanding of the rich possibilities for healing.

If dialogue is so critical for our well-being and existence, how can we recover a dialogue that has been lost through the death of a loved one? How can we transform an absence into a presence? The answer is by vitalizing our urge to communicate with our developing imagination. In this way, we gain access directly to the beloved.

INTERNAL COMMUNICATION

How, specifically, can we make that dreamed-of contact? Simply exhorting you to use your imagination is too vague. An effective, easy-to-learn method exists to enable you to reach the presence within. Internal communication is a powerful tool that utilizes the imagination to resolve old hurts and resentments, express love, adjust the relationship to its new context and circumstances, and feel more at peace with deceased loved ones. Such communication takes place inside you, opening up significant possibilities for the relationship that actually go far beyond the scope of the sort of everyday, external communication you are used to.

Communication is the single greatest factor affecting our relationships with family members. Not only for practical reasons and to keep the family running smoothly, but for our health and well-being, it is critical that we express our love, work through our anger and differences, and resolve particularly disturbing issues with those we cherish. For many people, however, the greater the difficulties within their relationships, the harder it is to talk freely. In most families, certain important issues and past events just aren't discussed, with members considering it unsafe to express, disagree about, or even confront the truth. Family therapist Virginia Satir writes in *Peoplemaking* that only 4.5 percent of the population is emotionally honest in their communications with family members; the rest cover up their true feelings, creating distance and mistrust in their relationships, undermining their self-worth, and building anxiety and stress.

But, as you will experience soon, encounters using internal communication techniques differ greatly from encounters in everyday life. Even if you are among those who resist full external communication, you will find that freely expressing yourself internally is not only possible but enjoyable. Here, inside, you can address unresolved aspects of a relationship—not merely a relationship with a deceased person but with anyone. You can voice repressed feelings, deepen bonds, heal rifts, and feel more compassion for the other person, all in privacy, without the other person's external presence. You'll learn to "step inside" the other person to gain valuable insights into the other's feelings and point of view. When you practice internal communication with the person you have lost, you'll experience the release of what has been bottled up inside and be more at peace with the loss as the love you feel begins to flow freely to its object.

As with any communications technique, the quality of internal communication depends on certain commitments from you:

- The resolve to proceed
- The promise to listen carefully as well as to speak out
- The willingness to take responsibility for your own feelings and avoid blaming, insulting, manipulating, and demanding

If you have hurts or resentments you want to communicate, be prepared to slow down and describe these so that your loved one can understand. If you feel angry, it will be most effective if you are specific. When it is your turn to listen, try to be as receptive, relaxed, and empathetic as you can. Ask thoughtful questions so that you can better understand the other's point of view. Acknowledge the feelings underlying the words as well as the content. This interaction is not a power struggle, and the point is not to prove right or wrong but to reopen, exchange, listen, weigh, and see old issues with fresh eyes.

In communication with the deceased, changing old patterns of interacting may not be as hard as it sounds. You may be surprised to discover that the person, and the relationship, too, as experienced in the imagination, have changed greatly. For example, in the physical body, the person may appear younger, healthier, and more vital than when alive; in the personality, the person may act with less ego, more compassion, and more objectivity and may be less likely to get caught up in family dynamics; in values and perspectives, old interests, even ones that were consuming passions in life, may have evaporated, and more concern for spiritual matters may be in evidence.

One of my clients, Doreen, found in a dream shortly after her father, Robert's, death that he had changed dramatically. Robert looked healthy and vital, though when he died, his body had been ravaged by cancer. In the dream, he was surrounded by the family, each member desperately asking financial questions about the estate. This made sense, since Robert had been very involved in investing and controlling the family finances, and the family still looked to him for advice and guidance. However, now he seemed completely disinterested. Waving all the questions aside, he said, "These things don't concern me now."

Later, in the chapter on technique, I'll suggest how such changes can help create breakthroughs in communication that seemed impossible before. For now, simply ready yourself to be open and receptive to changes in your loved one and to let yourself relinquish old pictures of the relationship.

It is important, too, that you approach internal communication free of preconceived ideas of the content and outcome of each encounter, since expectations can limit the vast range of the imagination. More often than not, the interactions with deceased loved ones will differ markedly from what you anticipate. Most people are pleasantly surprised both by what they discover in their inner encounters and, later, by outer events in their daily lives.

Consider Joseph, who was devastated by his brother Jim's death. The two had had a stormy relationship, and Jim's death appeared to end any possibility for reconciliation. When I suggested in a therapy session that Joseph use internal communication to gain access to his ongoing relationship with Jim, he was very skeptical. He assumed that he would be incapable of using his imagination effectively and that, even if he could reach Jim through his imagination, his brother would be as antagonistic as he had always been in life. Reluctantly, Joseph tried the exercise described in chapter 3. He was surprised not only by how vividly he saw Jim in his imagination but also by the warmth and love with which his brother greeted him. The two spoke at length about their relationship, a conversation that Joseph had longed for all his adult life, and Jim shared some childhood resentments that had poisoned his feelings for Joseph, resentments that stemmed from their parents' clear favoring of Joseph. After completing this exercise, Joseph not only felt loving and forgiving toward Jim, but sensed a new comfort in himself that felt significant and permanent.

TIMELESS REWARDS

The great Chilean-American novelist, Isabel Allende, told her publisher that she felt her writing career would end when her mother died, since her mother had always edited all her books. Her publisher reminded her that her mother was already inside her. Wrote Allende, "I realized he's right. Absolutely right. I will always be able to say, Okay, here I have a terrible sentence and my mother will come back to me . . . I hope that when I die I will have been able to, during my life, plant little seeds in the souls of my children and my grandchildren so that when they need something from me I will always be available" (Epel, p. 23). How comforting to have this understanding before a loved one's death! I have seen many others make similar breakthroughs and achieve life-changing insights by reaching the beloved within, healing old wounds, bringing the relationship up to date, and finally saying good-bye.

Succeeding chapters guide you in putting internal communication into practice. We begin simply, with exercises designed to help you express whatever has been concealed, held back, or repressed. Gradually, you will learn to have inner dialogues with the person you are missing. In part III, you'll learn to use internal communication techniques to ease communication problems with grieving family members.

It is never too late to reconcile with a loved one, whether living or dead. One eighty-two-year-old woman used the techniques described in this book to heal old wounds in her relationship with her father. He had died more than forty years before. The ways of imagining and communicating introduced here are gifts you will carry forever. Open yourself to them, reflect on them with patience and trust, and allow the possibility that they will work for you as you hope they will. The results could ease your pain and enrich your life forever.

PART 2

Reaching Within

*The communication of the dead is tongued with fire
beyond the language of the living.*

T. S. ELIOT

CHAPTER 2

Communicating With One Who Is Dying

Deena quietly entered the stark hospital room and took a seat next to her mother's bed. Although it had been just a few days since her last visit, Deena was shocked at how emaciated her mother looked, her pale skin drawn tightly over the protruding bones of her face. She was sleeping, her labored breathing suggesting that pain was disturbing her rest. It was still hard for Deena to comprehend that this frail and helpless person was her mother. When Deena was a child, the outspoken and energetic Angela had seemed larger than life. Deena had adored Angela for these qualities, though as a teenager she had abhorred them. From the time she turned twelve, Deena was embarrassed to be seen with her mother in public, feeling hypercritical of the way her mother dressed, talked, and walked . . . everything! It was then that Deena stopped talking to her mother about anything that really mattered to her. Mother and daughter fought viciously during those years. Eventually, they learned to relate cordially though distantly, but the original closeness never returned.

Now Angela was dying of breast cancer. Deena longed to talk to her, sharing her disappointments and joys and expressing her love. As Deena thought about this seeming impossibility, Angela stirred beneath the white sheets and opened her eyes. For a few precious minutes, she looked tenderly into her daughter's face. Deena reached for her mother's hand, pressing the cool, bony flesh into her own. "I'm here, Mom. I've missed you. I . . ." Her voice trailed off as she perceived that Angela suddenly seemed to be staring through her, as though some invisible presence had once again drawn away her mother's attention. Frustrated, Deena felt her chest tighten. She had really hoped to *talk* to her mother on this visit. There was so much she wanted to share with her: regrets, appreciations, recent realizations about their relationship, love.

Still staring into the distance, her mother softly mumbled, "I'm going on a trip soon. I need to get ready." This statement confused Deena. What was her mother talking about? She had made such statements before. Why did she keep telling her that she was going on a trip? She was too sick to even think about traveling! Last week when Angela had made a similar statement, Deena had tried to reason with her. "You're in the hospital, Mom. You need to save your energy for trying to get better." Angela had become very agitated, pulling at the sheets and trying to get out of bed. This time, so as not to upset her mother again, Deena remained silent.

Sitting with a family member who is in the final stages of dying can be excruciating, especially when one thinks about all that has never been said. Both the caring family members and the dying person may feel the urgent need to reconcile and yet still be unable to communicate in anything but short, unsatisfactory fragments. Too little energy, too little time—the sheer physical limits often defeat the most intense desire. Deena knew that her time to talk with her mother was quickly running out. Even when Angela was awake and aware, she only could focus for brief periods. Still, both knew instinctively that using what little time and energy were left to express love to each other could produce some of life's most meaningful moments. Simply the mutual urge to try was a healing bond between them.

HOW THE DYING COMMUNICATE

It can come as a surprise to the living, but communication is a critical part of the dying process. And yet communication with people on their deathbeds can be frustrating, confusing, and disorienting. Dying people seem absorbed in another realm, drifting in and out of contact with the living. When they look at us, their eyes are often glassy, unfocused; sometimes they seem to look right through us. People close to death may converse with invisible beings—perhaps dead friends or relatives—and speak of invisible places. Henri Nouwen, reflecting on his time with his dying mother, wrote in *In Memoriam*, "She was seeing other realities, more awesome, more frightening, more captivating, but also more decisive" (Nouwen, p. 22). Those who are dying may talk in symbols and act frustrated and restless when we cannot understand them. In the days before my father went into a coma, he tried constantly to get out of the hospital bed "to go home." I thought at that time that "home" meant my parents' house, some thirty minutes from the hospital. Now I realize that he meant something much more subtle—the return to a source.

Maggie Callanan and Patricia Kelly are hospice nurses who have written an important book on communicating with the dying called *Final Gifts*. They challenge the common assumptions that the dying are "out of it" or "confused," maintaining that these responses only serve to create more distance between the dying and their family and friends. These two pioneers carefully researched their patients' communications and realized that the dying often use symbolic language to describe what they are experiencing and express the wish for a peaceful death. Callanan and Kelly insist that if we pay close attention to everything the dying person says and does, we may begin to understand the messages. Cicely

Saunders, a founder of the hospice movement in England, wrote, "I once asked a man who knew he was dying what he needed above all from those caring for him. He said 'For someone to look at me as if they were trying to understand me' " (Saunders, p. 3).

To help make these last, precious opportunities for interaction rich with meaning and understanding, I offer the following suggestions for communicating with a dying loved one.

- Pay close attention to whatever a dying person says or does, since he or she may be trying to communicate an important message to you.
- Validate what the person is saying to you, even if you don't completely understand the message. Learn to listen without judging. Look for signs of frustration or agitation that may indicate you are misinterpreting the message.
- Let your loved one know when you are confused. Ask questions that reflect a genuine desire to understand what the dying person is experiencing. Give reassurance that you understand how difficult it is for the person to communicate with you.
- Watch for nonverbal cues. These may be very subtle. The dying person may squeeze your hand, raise an eyebrow, tighten muscles, breathe faster or slower, or make a sound.
- If you feel at a loss for words, or if words seem to get in the way of a deeper connection, simply sit with the person in silence. Much can be communicated through a reassuring and loving touch. You can also speak silently through your heart.

Just as the dying person may feel an urgency to communicate to you, so you may feel an urgency to communicate back in order to reconcile your relationship, express love, and resolve old hurts. Don't let the chance pass you by. Transcend any natural reticence or embarrassment you may feel to speak clearly, heartfully, and concisely. But be careful not to impose subjects on the person that you sense are too painful or uncomfortable. You can explore these matters later, on your own, using internal communication.

Because time is short and the actual exchanges you manage may be frustrating or unsatisfying, it can be helpful to work with internal communication even at the deathbed. As I sat next to my father in the hospital, I wanted to talk about his dying since this had stirred up so many feelings about our relationship. But from the moment he heard that he had cancer, he had refused to talk about dying. At first this caused me anguish, but I learned to talk with him about these topics in my imagination, resolving many of the resentments and hurts that had kept my heart so closed and protected in our adult relationship. Through this practice, I was able to be fully present, relaxed, and loving with my father in his last days. Before I attained these new possibilities for communication, I felt tense and expectant whenever I was with him, waiting and hoping for the right moment to talk about our relationship. But after talking with him in my imagination, I felt at peace just sitting with him in silence. My work with imagination during this time had given me a priceless gift.

The series of exercises and suggestions that follow will help you explore ways of communicating internally with a dying person. Feel free to do all the exercises in the order they are presented or just try the ones that you feel most drawn to. To get the best results, set aside an uninterrupted time in a special place. Think of this retreat place—a room in your own home—as a sanctuary. Choose a place where you feel safe and secure and where you can be alone. Set up an altar there with pictures, special objects, or drawings of the person who is dying.

So that you won't be interrupted, put a note on the door

and take your phone off the hook. Then, sit down before your altar, close your eyes, and focus on your breathing for a few minutes to settle your body and mind. Reserve thirty minutes to an hour for performing each exercise, doing only one per session. When you have completed each exercise, write down what happened to provide a record of events, help you integrate any insights, and give you the opportunity later to observe and interpret the changes occurring within yourself.

The sanctuary, though simple in concept, is a very potent place of healing. For years, my clients have retreated to their sanctuaries as a profoundly significant part of their process of coping with the dying and death of people close to them. Even after only a week of using the sanctuary, clients consistently report feeling more at peace, less overwhelmed by their emotions, and more able to attend to other obligations in their lives.

If you visit your sanctuary at least once a week (with more visits as you feel the need), it will be much easier to shift gears from the external world and focus on internal communication. Visiting it every week will build concentration while maintaining a sense of continuity.

EXERCISE 1

Internal Communication with the Dying

Relaxed in your sanctuary, close your eyes, and in your mind's eye visualize entering the room of the person who is dying. Sit down next to the bed. Take a few minutes to experience this room with all your senses. What do you see around you? What can you hear? Are there any smells? Take the person's hand and feel its weight, its temperature, and its texture. With a squeeze of the hand or with your words, let him or her know that you have come to visit. You now have the opportunity to communicate with this person in a way that you never really considered possible before. You can express everything that you want to in order to help resolve conflicts in your relationship. Picture yourself expressing your love and appreciation as well as your disappointments, regrets, and hurts. Then, in your imagination, listen carefully and respectfully to what your loved one has to say to you. Continue your dialogue until it feels complete. You may then want to spend some time together in silence. When you feel ready to leave, say good-bye and leave the room. Open your eyes, and savor your feelings for a few minutes. Then record your experience in the journal reserved for this purpose.

DEENA'S EXPERIENCE

Deena consulted with me during the period in which Angela was dying. She realized how important it was to share with Angela the love, appreciations, and disappointments she had held back for so many years. For more than thirty years, mother and daughter had avoided talking about their relationship. Too many times they had been silent about the little hurts and misunderstandings that had built up, as such impediments inevitably do, between two people. Ironically, just as Deena was beginning to feel ready to communicate with her mother, Angela began losing the ability to maintain contact for any length of time. Discussing her predicament with me, Deena expressed her frustration. She had hoped for the relief of finally having her say.

When I introduced the concept of internal communication, Deena saw immediately that channels of communication were open to her that she had not considered before.

She agreed to try the exercise above, and saw that it offered an opportunity to work through her own unresolved issues so that she could sit with Angela peacefully and lovingly as she died. Here's the account Deena wrote in her exercise journal of her experience in performing the exercise.

I entered the room. The late afternoon light was streaming across the bed, illuminating the form of Mother's frail body under the white blanket. She was wide awake, which surprised me. Her gray green eyes were fixed lovingly on me. I sat down next to her, stroked her hand, and told her, "Mother, I want to take this time to really talk with you. I regret we haven't for so many years. How hard it's been for me now that I'm so ready to talk to you and you just haven't been able to. I've come into your room many times lately full of resolve to tell you what weighs on my heart. And after just a few moments you will drift off. It's so hard for me to see you dying. Mother, what am I going to do without you?" I began to cry and my mother squeezed my hand and nodded. I knew that she understood my feelings.

I felt encouraged to go on. "When I was a little girl, I dreamed of growing up like you. I adored you. It seemed that you could do no wrong. Mother, we stopped talking when I was a teenager. That was such a difficult time for us. I criticized you constantly. I didn't listen to you. I talked back. I fought relentlessly with you. I needed to push you away at that time so that I could grow up. We were so close and I identified so much with you. I had to find who I was, separate from you. I want you to know that I never stopped loving you, even though I stopped expressing it. I still appreciate those qualities that I adored in you when I was a little girl. I wouldn't be who I am without all the wonderful qualities you instilled in me."

My mother was crying now, tears flooding her pale cheeks. We were both speechless as we looked into each other's eyes. I felt vulnerable and raw. I let my love show. For moments, I felt transported into a sacred time and space, where love flowed freely and fully. After a long while, my mother spoke quietly: "I love you so much, Deena. It broke my heart when you pulled away from me, when we stopped talking to one another. I didn't know what to do. My pride got in the way. And then I got used to the way we related. I forgot how wonderful it had been to hold you, to stroke your hair, to answer all your questions about life. I've missed out on much of our adult relationship. But I don't think that our relationship ends here. Perhaps we'll be closer from now on, even after I've died." I took my mother in my arms, sobbing with relief. The wall had come down. When I sat up again, the room had grown quite dark. The sun had set. Mother's eyes closed as she peacefully drifted into sleep. I kissed her on her forehead and quietly left the room.

When she opened her eyes, Deena was astounded by what had taken place. She had not expected the experience to feel so real. She told me that she felt relieved. Expressing what had been bottled up inside and having a meaningful talk with Angela within herself extinguished the urgency she had felt about talking with her mother in the hospital room.

In our next session, Deena had just come from her mother's bedside. Angela had been comatose, her eyes open but unseeing, and she was totally unresponsive to Deena's presence. Deena told me that this change in her mother's condition would have been devastating to her if she had not had the internal conversation recounted above. Now she felt comforted not only by that episode but by the thought that she could continue communicating with Angela on this level throughout her dying and after her death.

TALKING THROUGH THE HEART

Many times I talked to my father silently through my heart, a powerful technique I learned from Stephen Levine, author of *Who Dies?* Levine has observed that agitated people are able to quiet down and those in a coma can soften when the person next to them sends love and understanding through the heart. During such transmissions, it is not words that are important but the acceptance and care generated from within.

Levine stresses the discrimination we should use in talking through the heart, taking care not to impose our own needs, desires, or agendas on the dying person, even when we are sure we know what's best for that individual. He illustrates this point in *Who Dies?* with this story: A nurse, after learning from Levine the technique of talking through the heart, tried it with a difficult patient who refused to acknowledge that he was dying. A few times a day she would go into his room and talk silently to him through her heart about how he should accept death, not deny it. Finally, the head nurse told her that the patient had requested that she not go in his room anymore. When the nurse asked why, the head nurse responded, "He said you talk too much."

Talking silently through the heart can work at a distance as well as at a bedside. Sonja was caught up in a family drama that involved not telling her father that he was dying of cancer. Unfortunately, in maintaining this secret, she felt she could only talk to him on a superficial level, which was very painful when there was so much more she wanted to discuss. I suggested she try talking to him through her heart, even though he was thousands of miles away. Sonja was doubtful that this could have any effect but tried it anyway. She told her father that she knew he had cancer, that she wanted him to live, but that she was willing to let him go if that was best for him.

After a few weeks, Sonja felt calmer and more at peace with the situation. Then she had a dream in which her father told her, "I know what the doctors won't tell me. I'm all right, so don't worry about me. Remember to put oil in your car and get your tires changed every thirty thousand miles."

With this message, Sonja realized that she no longer needed to obsess about her father; rather, she needed to focus on the basic mechanics of living her own life. When she visited him in the hospital shortly thereafter, she was the only family member who was able to sit quietly with him and accept his situation with grace.

EXERCISE 2

Connecting Through Your Heart

Sit down and close your eyes. For a few minutes, bring your full attention to the pattern of your breathing. Feel the breath passing through your nostrils. Then focus on the heart center on the sternum between your breasts. Be aware of any sensations there, no matter how subtle they may be. You may want to touch that area with your fingers. Once your attention is centered there, breathe in and out of your heart.

Now, begin to talk to your loved one through your heart: silently, gently, truthfully, compassionately. The words flow through your heart on the waves of your breath. You may want to say that you are fully present, that you care, that you want to support the person in the passage, that you will miss the person when death occurs. Or you might simply send love through your heart. Maintain the physical connection with the heart as you silently speak.

COMMUNICATING WITH A COMATOSE PERSON

There comes a time when a dying person slips into a dreamless state and is no longer responsive to other people or to the environment. Then, communication as we have known it is no longer possible, but internal communication techniques, including talking through the heart, can serve to maintain a connection. If you have been practicing these techniques throughout a loved one's illness, you will not feel as cut off when coma occurs. Internally, you will experience a bridge of communication.

In his brilliant book *Coma*, psychiatrist Arnold Mindell proposes that many people in comatose states are actually in an altered state of consciousness and that it is possible to reach them if we can learn a more refined way of communicating. Mindell listens and watches carefully, acknowledges when he is confused, asks questions, and validates the person's experience. In this way, Mindell is able to engage in a meaningful dialogue that explores any conflicts the person may be experiencing about dying.

After introducing himself, Mindell sits close to the person in a coma, touching the person's wrist or hand, and pacing his own breathing with that of the patient. He next affirms the internal experience of the comatose person, commenting on events that are not apparent to the observer: "Whatever is happening, whatever it is, will show us the way. It is going to be our guide. So continue to feel, see, hear and move with the feelings, visions, sounds, and movements happening within you. This will bring you wherever we have to go" (p. 30). Mindell then looks for subtle cues of response such as spasms, twitches, facial movements, the opening or focusing of the eyes, and changes in the person's breathing. In this way, communication is established. Mindell maintains that he has "not met anyone who has not responded to [this] kind of interaction."

In *Coma*, he describes an eighty-year-old patient, John, who had been in a semicomatose state for six months. At the point that Mindell was called in, John was intensely agitated, shouting and groaning. As I mentioned before, dying people who feel they are misunderstood often become agitated, a concept Mindell fully comprehended and affirmed. He sat down next to John and began to breathe and groan along with him. Even though this man had not spoken a complete sentence for months, a dialogue developed. In broken short phrases, John announced that a big ship was coming for him. With Mindell asking questions that reflected a genuine desire to understand what John was experiencing, John revealed that he was not going to take this ship. John became even more agitated at this point, and Mindell sensed that their dialogue was getting close to the heart of some conflict John had about dying. Mindell continued to ask questions that helped John explore this conflict.

John told him that this ship was coming to take him on vacation, but that he had never taken a vacation and felt that he had to go back to work. Mindell encouraged John to explore the ship and report back to him about what he found. John described angels driving the ship. The trip was also free. With this information, Mindell encouraged John to take the vacation. He could come back or continue on if he wanted to. John's last words were: "Yeah. Yeah. Vacation to the Bahamas. Ba . . . ha . . . mas. Yeah. Hmmm. No work." At this point, John fell into a peaceful sleep and died a half hour later.

Mindell is gifted in initiating verbal dialogues with comatose people who had previously seemed incapable of talking. With some patients, however, he must rely on nonverbal communication, watching for cues such as changes in breathing or subtle body movements; for example, in the mouth, eyes, eyebrows, or hands. If any such movements occur consistently in response to a stimulus, they could suggest a means of communication. One comatose client made slight eyebrow movements in response to Mindell's statements. These were enough to enable Mindell to comprehend the person's messages.

The dialogue with John demonstrates the symbolic nature of communication with the dying. Crossing a river or going on a journey are metaphors often used by the dying to describe their experience of crossing over. In *On Dreams and Death*, Marie-Louise Von Franz writes, "In my experience the image of the journey in dreams is also the most frequently occurring symbol of impending death" (Von Franz, p. 64). For John, dying was a journey—and a deeply disturbing prospect, since he had never taken a vacation from work.

Malby, a seventy-year-old man, also had conflicts about dying. Three days before he fell and sustained a fatal injury to the head, he had a vivid dream that he promptly shared with his daughter, Kathleen. "I went across the Rio Grande looking for Ruth. I couldn't find her, so I came back." Ruth was his ex-wife; they had been divorced for more than thirty years, with little communication. However, when Ruth was dying of bone cancer, Malby became very concerned and wanted to visit her. It was just before the trip was arranged that he fell and hit his head, causing severe hemorrhage to his brain. His statement suggested that he may have wanted to meet his ex-wife in death. He was the first to venture over the Rio Grande, but she was not ready to meet him, so Malby didn't die immediately, as was expected by the doctors. He slipped into a coma that lasted five days.

Realizing Malby's conflict, Kathleen talked to him while he was comatose, assuring him that many other deceased loved ones would be there for him, and that Ruth would be meeting him soon. Malby died peacefully, followed two days later by Ruth. This story reminded me of how significant a past relationship can become to the dying, even one that has seemingly faded in outward importance over the years. Kathleen had the sensitivity to Malby without making judgments about what *she* thought was important. Knowing her parents' history of divorce and animosity, she could have easily dismissed Malby's statement about looking for Ruth. However, though she didn't really understand, she was willing to listen to and support her father in his quest to meet Ruth again.

In a deeply moving and now well-known example, Isabel Allende's daughter became ill and then fell into a coma. Certain that Paula would eventually awaken, her mother sought to maintain communication with her daughter by writing a long letter, published as Allende's memoir, *Paula*. "Listen, Paula," the book begins. "I am going to tell you a story, so that when you wake up you will not feel so lost." With sensitivity and humor, Allende records the family history and expresses her own fears and emotions as she cares for her unresponsive daughter. Months later, she has a vision/dream in which her daughter speaks to her: "Listen, Mama, wake up. I don't want you to think you're dreaming. I've come to ask for your help . . . I want to die and I can't. I see a radiant path before me, but I can't take that first step, something is holding me. All that's left in my bed is my suffering body, degenerating by the day; I perish for thirst and cry out for peace, but no one hears me. I am so tired! . . . The only thing holding me back a little is having to go alone; if you took my hand it would be easier to cross to the other side— the infinite loneliness of death frightens me. Help me one more time, Mama. You've fought like a lioness to save me, but reality is overpowering you. It's all useless now . . . I have lived my time and I want to say good-bye . . . After I die, we will stay in contact that way you do with your grandparents and Granny; I will be in you as a constant, soft presence, I will come when you call, communication will be easier when you don't have the misery of my sick body before you and you can see me as I was in the good days" (Allende, p. 315). This vision/dream was a turning point for Allende. She realized that her daughter was not going to wake up and that she now needed to help her die rather than fight for her life. Almost a year after becoming comatose, Paula died in her mother's arms "with the same perfect grace that characterized all the acts of her life" (Allende, p. 325). Writing the letter sustained Allende throughout the devastating months of her daughter's coma and prepared her for her daughter's death.

As we gain more understanding of what a comatose person is experiencing, we are less likely to treat this person as though he or she is not there. It has been a common practice in hospitals to talk insensitively around comatose people, on the assumption that they can hear nothing. Yet, many stories are recounted in the near-death literature of those who awakened from a coma and gave detailed accounts of doctors' conversations and procedures.

A client, Jason, shared an unnerving experience he had had in the hospital with his comatose father, Ben. One afternoon, a nurse checked on Ben's vital signs and then proclaimed to Jason in Ben's presence that Ben was in the final stages of dying and probably would not last past midnight. No sooner had the words left her mouth than Ben bolted upright, glared at the nurse, and then sank back down into the bed. As though to spite the nurse, he held on past midnight and passed away the next afternoon.

When you feel that communication has broken down with a person in a coma, try to follow the suggestions of Arnold Mindell, which were discussed on page thirty-six. In addition, write your loved one a letter (chapter 4 returns to this idea in more detail) or use exercises 1 and 2 from this chapter. All these methods will help you maintain a connection with the person who appears to be unresponsive.

WHEN DEATH OCCURS IN YOUR ABSENCE

Some of my clients' deepest regrets stem from being absent at the moment of their loved ones' deaths. They feel that they have missed the opportunity to say good-bye, express love, and spend those last irreplaceable moments together. Some people simply take a short break from the bedside, only to find that the person has died while they were gone. Some are en route to the hospital and arrive too late. Others have no warning because the person died suddenly. These absences inspire an array of feelings: anger, guilt, regret, sadness, or a combination of these. Particularly where the death is violent or results from suicide or an accident, those left behind can suffer profound emotional distress as they go over and over the details of their last encounter with the deceased and picture possible scenarios of what the dying person experienced.

The same techniques that foster communication can help you place yourself at the scene of your loved one's death. If you are uncomfortable about where the death took place, you can choose another, more soothing environment. Again, as with previous exercises involving imagery, it is important to experience this place with all your senses. In your imagination, sit with the person who is dying. Express what is in your heart; say good-bye. Be open to any last words your loved one may want to communicate to you, and remember to say "I love you." Exercise 3 will help you use your imagination to experience in detail the passing of a loved one who has died in your absence.

EXERCISE 3

Imagining a Loved One's Passing

In your sanctuary, sit down and close your eyes. Let go of all distractions and concerns and bring your full attention to the internal landscape of your imagination. Imagine that you are sitting beside the person who is dying. What do you see? Smell? Hear? What are you feeling? Be aware of the sound of the person's breathing. Is it smooth or labored? Light or heavy? Synchronize your breathing to his or her breathing so that you are breathing in and out together.

You are participating in a sacred time of transition, sharing the last moments of a life. Now is the time to express your love, whether through words or touch. Are there any unresolved issues you want to bring up? Listen carefully. Does the person want to speak to you? Explore any resistance you feel about letting go of this person, but since letting go may take days, weeks, or months, don't worry about completing this process before going on to the next part of the exercise.

When you are ready, reassure the person that he or she can move on now. Say good-bye. Be fully present and aware of the last breath. This marks the end of a lifetime and the end of your relationship as you have known it. After death has occurred, take time to sit with the body, reflecting on what has just happened and on your loss. Allow yourself to fully experience the impact; cry if you need to. Now that you have participated fully in your loved one's passing, contemplate your own feelings. Notice any subtle changes in the loved one's body as time passes. You might also become aware of the person's spirit.

When you feel ready, prepare to leave. Open your eyes, and record what you have experienced.

REGRET AND GUILT

Christina was very disappointed that she was not at her mother's side when she died, and she could not stop feeling miserable that her mother, Bette, had died alone. During

one of our sessions, I guided her via her imagination to the
hospital where Bette had died. Sitting beside the frail body,
Christina took Bette's hand. It was cold and slightly stiff, but
Christina could feel an almost imperceptible squeeze. Weep-
ing, she told Bette how much she loved her.

As Christina reassuringly held her mother's hand, her
mother's breaths grew shorter and more labored. Suddenly
she opened her eyes and looked at Christina with indescrib-
able love. Just as quickly, Bette's eyes closed again and, with
one more breath, she died with a slight smile on her cracked
lips. Christina sobbed, deeply moved that she had shared
such a sacred and intimate moment with her mother. She
no longer felt the regret that had afflicted her grief.

Suzanne, who was also absent when her mother died, felt
a need to explore the questions and regrets she was left with
in her grief. She felt guilty about putting her mother in a
care home and had questions about what her mother experienced in the hospital during her final days and as she died.
In her journal, she wrote, "I'd like to be able to talk with
my mother, to ask her the questions I failed to ask during
her life and to be present with her now to make up for the
times I failed to be present with her in the past. . . . I plan
to hold a dialogue with my mother and to use my imagination
and my love to hear her answers."

Here is Suzanne's recording of that internal dialogue.

SUZANNE: Are you at peace, Mother?
MOTHER: Yes, but it's not the peace as you think of it.
    It's not calm passiveness. It's more acceptance and
    understanding.
SUZANNE: I always feel guilty that I did not have you
    come live with us after Daddy's death. It was so com-
    plicated. I thought we had lots of years. I wanted you
    to be fixed up in the care home near me, and I
    wanted you to become independent. I had the idea
    you could enjoy life now that Daddy wasn't there to

dominate you. I had plans for us to go on a cruise in the summer. Also, I was afraid of losing my independence if we lived together. It had been so hard won. When I imagined living with both you and Michael, I didn't see any room for me in the picture. I wondered how I could possibly meet both of your expectations, especially since they would probably be at odds. Was I terribly selfish?

MOTHER: I didn't understand, it's true. But we can only do what we can do at that time. I didn't hold it against you. I thanked God that I had you. What would I have done, and who would I have turned to, if you had not been there?

SUZANNE: How did you feel before you collapsed and were rushed to the hospital from the nursing home the last time?

MOTHER: I felt alone. I was depressed and discouraged. I couldn't understand how I had ended up there. I wanted to hold onto you, and I was angry—angry at my helplessness and my confusion. No one who worked there seemed to care. A little bit of kindness was the most valuable prize in the world then. I didn't want to burden you. I knew you had your life and your work. I just wanted you to hold me one more time. I wanted something familiar; I wanted to go home.

SUZANNE: Did you think of death?

MOTHER: Yes. "Home" was the key. I began to think of that time I had that experience in the hospital a long time ago.

SUZANNE: The near-death experience.

MOTHER: Yes. I wasn't afraid. And I remembered the way I felt—at peace. I decided that was going to be home for me now. That was the home I could get to. And I imagined your father on the other side. Waiting for me. I waited a long time to have you. I couldn't imagine your not being with me.

SUZANNE: Were you angry when you realized they had resuscitated you in the hospital? Were you aware or conscious at all during those nine days on life support?

MOTHER: I never wanted that to happen. But I died as I had lived, didn't I? Under a doctor's care. I knew you were with me every day. I knew you were there. I went in and out of consciousness. It was painful, but if it hadn't been that way, we would never have had that time. And that time was precious to me. It really was. I felt your love with me. When you left to go home for dinner that last day, I knew my time was up; I knew I would never see you again. I treasure the time we did have.

SUZANNE: I felt a sadness, a resistance from you, when I said good-bye. I assured you I would be back after dinner. I focused on that, because I didn't want to acknowledge to myself that anything other could be the case. You had so much care in the intensive unit. I was angry when they moved you to a regular floor. You didn't have the attention and care you should have had.

MOTHER: No, I didn't. No one seemed to care; I was just another body to bother with.

SUZANNE: When I came into the room after the call to come to the hospital, your body was just lying on the bed. No one had covered you. No one was there to tell me before I entered the room that you had died. I'm so glad Michael was with me. When I saw your body I said to Michael, "She's gone." And that is what it looked like to me. Your body didn't look like my mother. It was obvious to me that you weren't there anymore. That you'd gone.

MOTHER: I had gone, and it was with relief. But it was not without pain—the pain of separation more than physical pain. But it was, and I knew it was, the way it must be. Except for you, everyone who ever meant anything to me was dead. I did not go fearfully, but rather gratefully, to be with those I loved and to leave you to carry on your life. It was as it should have been. You don't need to have regrets. I loved you in holding on, and I love you in release. Live your life and live in love.

In reading over this dialogue, Suzanne felt very much in communication with her mother. She could feel her mother's presence and love, and her mother's words were consoling and validating. While she felt relieved in expressing the guilt, conflicts, and concerns she had experienced throughout her mother's illness, Suzanne also gained more understanding of what her mother was experiencing while she was dying: the shame, frustrations, fears, and peace.

Using internal communication, we can discover that death need not cut us off from those we love. By writing letters or dialogues like Suzanne's, or simply by talking through our hearts or working with imagery, we can find new potential for change and growth in our relationships with those who are dying and those who have died. Here's another bonus, too often unrecognized even by those who benefit from it: any breakthroughs or healing we experience with those who have died can enhance our capacity for meaningful and fulfilling relationships with those who are alive.

CHAPTER 3

Dreaming of One Who Has Died

It is in our dreams that many of us first experience an ongoing relationship with a loved one who has died. As we grieve, it is common to dream vividly of the person, and these dreams can shock us by how real they feel. In the first moments of awakening from such a dream, we are often confused and disoriented, wondering if the person really is still alive after all. And then, as we shift to waking consciousness, we realize that indeed this person has died. But the experience of having been with the person in a dream can comfort and reassure us with the knowledge that, in spite of our loss, he or she still lives on within us. Many people treasure these dreams, remembering them for the rest of their lives, and they look forward to the appearance of loved ones in future dreams in which the person will appear.

Such after-death dreams fall into several categories:

- Dreams that reassure the dreamer that, although death has occurred, the deceased is still accessible and is not suffering
- Dreams that demonstrate that the relationship with the dreamer has changed but not ended
- Dreams in which unresolved issues in the relationship either arise or are actively addressed

- Dreams in which the deceased gives the dreamer support or guidance

DREAMS OF REASSURANCE

Dreams of reassurance can be a great relief to those who are grieving. Often, the deceased demonstrates peacefulness and urges the dreamer not to worry. Interestingly, in most dreams it's the dreamer who has the greatest difficulty in adjusting to the death that has occurred, not the person who has died. As an example, after her father's death, Beth had the following dream:

In the most vivid dream of my life, I was walking with my father. I told him how upset I was that he had died and how good it was to see him again. He turned to me and, with a deep belly laugh, said, "But why are you upset? It's okay with me." I was relieved but told him that I was sad he wasn't with me anymore. He stopped walking, looked into my eyes, and said, "Bethy, of course I'm with you."

Shortly after her grandmother's death, Laura dreamed that her grandmother walked into the living room. Laura was comforted to see her again, but confused, too, because she knew that her grandmother had just died. Laura spoke: "I'm so overjoyed to see you again, but I thought that you had died." Her grandmother simply but firmly stated, "I never died." Laura awakened with the certainty that her relationship with her grandmother had not been severed by death.

DREAMS THAT CONFIRM A RELATIONSHIP

Many dreams confirm the fact that the connection with a loved one remains unsevered and that the relationship continues to unfold, despite the death of the body. Dreams can show death to have had a transforming effect on both the relationship and the person who has died. As though to emphasize the changes since death, the recently deceased often appear healthy, vital, and younger than when last seen in life.

Adrian sent me a dream she had had a year after her mother's death. For eleven years, her mother had been paralyzed, unable to walk, speak, read, or write, even though her mind remained clear. Caring for her mother trapped in a crippled body had been a heartbreaking experience for Adrian.

I see a large room with people seated in chairs near the walls, leaving the center free. I notice a woman walking briskly around the room, swinging her arms. She is wearing a long, loose dress, something like a nightgown. Then I recognize her—my mother! She looks directly at me, smiles, and waves.

Adrian considered this dream a message from her mother, communicating that she was now free of all physical limitations. When Adrian saw the radiant smile and happy wave, she knew her mother was happy. Even years later, thinking about this dream gave Adrian a sense of deep and comforting joy.

Flo also experienced a dramatic change in her parents via her dreams. Soon after her father's death, he appeared in two dreams in which his robust and youthful body radiated a bright white light. Flo was stunned by this transformation, since her father had been sick for most of her life. After these dreams, Flo felt confident that her father was not suffering in his after-death state. Ten years later, Flo's mother died after months of agonizing medical complications caused by failed heart surgery. After her death, Flo's mother appeared repeatedly in Flo's dreams.

My mom and I were so close we were just like sisters. We shared everything. She was a very giving, loving, sharing, nurturing kind of person. I wasn't really young when she died, but her death was still traumatic: a long process of dying that transpired over two and a half months of intensive care.

After mom died, I was convinced that she was going to appear to me and that I wouldn't be able to handle it. I just kept praying that she would come to me in my dreams, and that's what she did.

She was so different: she appeared as my teacher. I recognized her physically, but I didn't recognize her energy; it was completely different from what I had known. She would not allow me to refer to her as "my mother" or say that she was dead; if I did, she would disappear.

She was teaching me that in the afterlife she no longer identified herself as my mother; she had moved on and our relationship had changed. I felt a sense of freedom after these dreams. I knew that she had truly found herself because she had gone beyond what she was able to do in this lifetime—to put herself first at the risk of disappointing someone else. She was teaching me to accept myself *and* her. This made me aware of the ways I was limiting myself in my work, and in certain aspects of my relationships.

At first, Flo was disappointed in these dreams, for she missed the warm relationship she had known with her mother. But in the dreams, Flo's mother appeared in a way that encouraged Flo to take more risks in her own life and to have the courage to follow her heart.

Editor Beth Witrogen McLeod buried both her parents in the same year. When she visited her parents' condo for the last time, she discovered two cardinals, male and female, singing on the deck. Although she had never seen cardinals at the condo before, she thought of her parents immediately, since these were her parents' favorite birds. The synchroncity was confirmed for her by a dream in which her father kept repeating a phrase, "The red cardinal only comes out in the winter." Beth cried out, "So it *was* you at the condo!" to which her parents replied, laughing, "Yes, yes."

DREAMS OF UNRESOLVED ISSUES

In his memoir *Patrimony*, Philip Roth describes his decision to bury his father in a shroud, even though he knew that this would be out of character for his father. His father was not an Orthodox Jew, but rather a "sturdy man rooted all his life in everydayness." Six weeks after the burial, Roth dreamed that his father appeared in a white shroud, admonishing him, "I should have been dressed in a suit. You did the wrong thing" (Roth, p. 237).

It is very common for unresolved feelings to surface in dreams soon after a death, especially insights that were too frightening or threatening to face when the person was still alive. Personality flaws or weaknesses, family secrets, alcoholism, drug addiction, incidents of incest—all such repressed material may come to light.

In *Bradshaw On: The Family*, John Bradshaw refers to the family trance, an unquestioned view of reality shared by the members of a family. Bradshaw shows how this trance is broken by "leaving home, growing up, breaking the bond with Mother." This trance can also be shattered when a family member, particularly a parent, dies. It is then that we can begin to recognize the constrictive conditioning we grew up with and gain insight into issues we may have previously overlooked.

Our dreams inform us of the presence of these unaddressed issues and offer guidance into healing. When we ignore such dreams, they often repeat themselves. If we continue to ignore them, they can develop into nightmares. Gale reported having persistent nightmares of the dying of her father who had passed away when Gale was an adolescent. Gale awakened upset from these dreams, unable to shake off the images of her father's suffering. She had not grieved when he died or since, and had never believed that she needed to. But the nightmares signaled the presence of her unresolved grief at a time when she could face it in therapy. As Gale began to grieve actively, her dreams gave her images of a father increasingly healthy. The more she healed, the healthier he became. Finally, when this phase of grieving had been completed, her father stopped appearing. However, note that I said this *phase* of grieving: we are never completely over grief, and it is normal for it to resurface from time to time. I cautioned Gale to expect her father to appear again in future dreams, most likely at times when her grief became active once more.

In another example, soon after Paul's mother's death, he had repeated dreams in which his mother appeared drunk, staggering about the room and slurring her words. These dreams drove home the fact that she had indeed been alcoholic, a problem that the family had avoided facing when she was alive.

When all the family members are alive, the family system is carefully held in place. When one of the members dies, the system is thrown into a chaotic state, destabilizing each family member. Old ways of coping are no longer effective; those left behind feel exhausted, losing their enthusiasm for living. This exhaustion, combined with a sense of disorientation and disillusionment, makes room for new awarenesses to break into consciousness—awarenesses that at other times a person could keep at bay.

In his grief, Paul could no longer sustain his denial of his mother's alcoholism; through his dreams, he could see it clearly. At first, he felt overwhelmed by this new awareness and resisted letting go of the more comforting image of his mother. However, in his grief support group, Paul was relieved to hear that others also had had disturbing insights after a family member's death. With the support and encouragement of the group members, he learned to talk about his inner turmoil and to educate himself about adult children of alcoholics.

Conversely, some dreams may bring home the painful

knowledge that the dreamer failed to appreciate or honor the positive qualities of the person who died. A client named Tom reported in a session that he hadn't liked his brother, Robert, very much when he was alive. Whenever Tom spent time with Robert, he felt so irritated by the latter's personality quirks that he would think to himself, "If Rob raises his eyebrow at me one more time, if he speaks in that tone anymore, I'm going to scream." Tom never did scream, but he felt so tense after each visit that he avoided contact with his brother as much as possible. After one lengthy separation, his brother died suddenly of a heart attack. Though devastated, Tom was relieved when Robert appeared in a dream a few weeks after his death. He stood silently before Tom, smiling broadly, his eyes fixed on Tom in a loving gaze. Ecstatic at seeing his brother, Tom felt overcome with a deep love for him. In the dream, he suddenly realized how sincere and caring his brother had been, qualities he had never noticed when his brother was alive. After the dream, Tom continued to explore this new relationship through imagery exercises.

A dramatic dream opened the way for a woman I will name Rose to appreciate and honor her father in a way that had been impossible when he was alive, because she hadn't known that he was her father. In the months before this man died, Rose had learned some startling information about her mother and had just begun to explore the possibility that a close family friend was actually her father. She had intended to have a talk with him about this, for she felt confident that he knew the truth. However, he died before this talk could take place. Shortly thereafter, Rose had a significant dream in which she held this man in her arms as he was dying. He looked up at her tenderly and said, "My darling daughter." "So you really believe I am your daughter?" Rose asked. "Of course," he replied. Knowing that in the dream her father was going to die in her arms, Rose awakened in a state of profound joy and peace.

Dreams can also highlight what is being repressed in the grieving process. Joseph dreamed about his wife, Lynne, a few months after her death. In the dream, Lynne was stretched out on a bed, looking very pale and weak. With great effort, she held out her hand to her husband. The tenderness of that gesture touched him so deeply that he awakened from the dream sobbing. The tears surprised him, for he had tried to maintain his composure since his wife's death. This dream had broken through his defenses, and now it felt good to let down and weep. Weeks later, his wife appeared again in a dream; this time she was healthy and contented.

DREAMS OF SUPPORT OR GUIDANCE

Many people who are grieving have dreams in which the deceased gives them support or guidance. In fact, sometimes the person seems more compassionate and insightful in death than in life.

In an interview, novelist Oscar Hijuelos described how his deceased father helped him through a particularly stressful period of his life. While working on his novel, *The Mambo Kings*, Hijuelos broke into a painful rash that seriously interfered with his writing. He felt that this rash erupted out of his guilt over exposing family secrets in his book. At the height of his crisis, Hijuelos had a dream in which his father tenderly washed him in a river. When he awakened, he had a strong sense of well-being, and the rash was gone. Hijuelos felt convinced that his father had given him his blessing to go ahead and write the book.

In chapter 1, I made reference to Doreen's dream about her father shortly after his death. This was the dream in which the family was gathered around her father. Her brothers and sisters were firing questions at him about the estate. The father, who in life had successfully managed and controlled the family money, was clearly annoyed by these questions and told the family, "These things don't concern me now." He then turned to Doreen, who was standing in the back of the room, and assured her in a soft but firm voice, "I've seen to it that your crops will not fail." Doreen was very moved by this dream, both by the dramatic change in her father's values and by his reassurance about her "crops." She felt perplexed by this statement but interpreted it to mean that her father was looking after her and that she would be able to provide well for herself. Many people report dreams in which the deceased loved one expresses a change in values or perspective, as the father in this dream did when he stated, "These things don't concern me now."

DREAMS OF THE DYING

The dreams of the dying can teach us of their conflicts and attempts to prepare for death. Careful attention to dreams may reveal to us unfinished business or fears about death that prevent people from dying in peace. Dream pioneer Marie-Louise Von Franz gives many case histories of clients whose dreams served as preparation for their deaths, but she also suggests that the unconscious itself does not embrace death but behaves as though the individual's psychic life will continue on. The unconscious, she believes, prepares consciousness not for a definite end, but for a transformation. In *The Way of the Dream*, Von Franz relates the dream of a dying woman in which a candle was slowly burning down on a windowsill. As the candle began to flicker, the woman began to panic, thinking that a great darkness was coming. At that moment, the candle suddenly appeared burning brightly on the sill on the other side of the window. Von Franz interprets this dream to mean: "Yes, the candle of your life is flickering. But life will continue in another medium, in another sphere. Beyond the isolating threshold of the window, that very same life will be going on" (Von Franz, p. 214).

This dream helped this woman reframe her understanding of death: she learned to see it not as a closed door but as a threshold experience. In nature, thresholds are phenomena that involve sudden changes in the form of matter—for example, the point at which a liquid freezes or a liquid evaporates. Death, writes Von Franz, may be such a threshold, involving a transformation of life as we have known it.

JEREMY'S DREAM

While there was no current crisis in his life, Jeremy consulted me because his work and personal life felt flat and meaningless. Exhausted most of the time, he no longer felt excited about anything. I encouraged him to bring a dream to therapy. At first, he insisted that he didn't dream. I asked him to set an intention to remember a dream before he went to sleep, to put a pad and pen by his bed, and, whenever he woke up, to immediately write down whatever he remembered about a dream, no matter how brief or seemingly insignificant. He brought a disturbing dream to our next session: sick horses were dying in a dark cellar. Without food, water, or light, some horses had already died. After briefly discussing the dream, I asked him to close his eyes and reenter the dream. In his imagination, he went back into the cellar.

When he did, he agonized over the horses' suffering. Surrounded by a stench of decomposing bodies, they huddled helplessly in the darkness. Whereas once they had feasted on golden hay brought by their owners, no one now came to feed or care for them. Suddenly, from a dark corner, Jeremy's mother stepped forward. She did not speak but tenderly extended her pale hand toward him.

When Jeremy opened his eyes again, we discussed what he had experienced. He was surprised by how easily he had been able to slip back into the dream. The horses had appeared as vividly as they had in his original dream. But he was perplexed by the appearance of his mother, which had not taken place in his dream.

His voice cracking and his face flushed with emotion, Jeremy spoke of his mother, who had died when he was five, leaving his father to struggle financially and the extended family to help as it could. Up to this point in psychotherapy, Jeremy had minimized the impact on him of this traumatic event from his childhood, even though his mother had been an attentive, loving, nurturing presence.

It occurred to Jeremy as he reflected on his dream that as the horses had been abandoned, so had he. And, as the horses were suffering, so was he. While Jeremy had not dreamed initially about his mother, the images of the decaying and dying horses were disturbing enough to bring the loss of her to consciousness. Immersing himself in the dream again through his imagination, he was able to make a connection between the state of the horses and his own unresolved grief. He wondered what would happen if he descended into the dark caverns of his grief and gave it his full attention for a period of time. Would his vitality return? When he talked about these insights in our next session, we focused on his buried grief, and this led to an outpouring of sadness. In poignant dialogues with his mother, Jeremy told her how helpless and alone he had felt when she died. He wept when his mother shared her deep sorrow in having to leave him and expressed her abiding love for him. In Jeremy's next dream, the horses were gone and the cellar was brightly furnished as a living room. Images of living had replaced the images of dying: Jeremy's unresolved grief was no longer draining the life force out of him.

Preparation Dreams

Dreams often help to prepare a person *before* a loss. For example, a client of mine dreamed that her mother told her, "I'm ready to join your father. Don't worry about me. I'll be fine." My client awakened in a state of profound peace that lasted for weeks. She knew that her mother was ready to die and that she would die soon, and her dream inspired her to spend as much time with her mother as she could during the last days of her life.

Writer Laurens van der Post recalls a dream in which his good friend Carl Jung stood at the garden gate, waving his hand and calling out to him, "I'll be seeing you." Jung died that night. Such dreams of an anticipated death can prepare and comfort a person, for they suggest that, even as we are on the brink of losing someone we love, a link with that person remains within the psyche that will not be broken by death.

While such dreams are readily understandable, others may be more opaque. I had a perplexing dream a year before my father's death. In the dream, I answered a knock on my hotel room door and my father stood silently, lovingly extending a white chrysanthemum toward me. There was something about this flower that I didn't want to accept, and I tried to close the door. I awakened from the dream feeling very agitated. It was only after the cancer diagnosis that I realized that the chrysanthemum was a funeral flower and that the dream had come to prepare me for my father's death. When I had the dream, no one knew that my father had or would develop cancer, although I now suspect that the cancer was already quietly present in his body. Even though I rejected the message of the dream at the time, I do feel in retrospect that the powerful image of the flower in my father's hand planted a seed in my psyche that would grow in time into an acceptance of my father's terminal diagnosis.

It is probable that many preparation dreams slip by unnoticed. You may awaken disturbed and confused by a dream that makes no sense to you now, but that could come to have deep meaning. For this reason, your dream journal can help you keep in touch not just with the dreams you are working with but with past dreams whose relevance may eventually be revealed. Had I not recorded the chrysanthemum dream in my dream journal, I would have forgotten it, and would never have made the connection between the flower and my father's illness.

Many people are comforted by preparation dreams, but others may experience them with distress, finding themselves left with a sense of dread, helplessness, or guilt. Jean dreamed that on a visit to the home of her sister, Ann, her sister seemed strangely, disturbingly detached. Suddenly it occurred to Jean that Ann was dead, but as Jean panicked, Ann laughed and counseled her not to worry.

Jean awakened shaking uncontrollably and drenched in sweat. She called Ann immediately and was relieved to hear her voice. However, the dream filled her with dread. Was Ann going to die? Was there anything she could do to prevent it? Afraid that speaking of her dream might make it come true, she pushed it into a dark corner of her psyche, where it festered for five months. Then one evening she received the phone call she had been dreading: Ann had died in a car accident. While Jean acknowledged that the dream did help her after her sister's death, she resented the distress she experienced for so many months beforehand.

If you have such a dream, treat it as a wake-up call. If we do not die first, we will witness the death of every one of our loved ones—perhaps soon, perhaps later. If your loved one were to die tomorrow, what would you regret? What would be left unsaid? What issues would be left unresolved? What can you do today to feel more at peace with that person and with yourself? Preparation dreams don't have to throw you into a frozen panic; in this way they can mobilize you to act now to bring healing into your relationships.

DREAMS AS GRIEF PROGRESSES

The first response to the death of a loved one is shock or denial. Unable to fully absorb the impact of the death that has just occurred, the mind and body respond with numbness. Edges are blurred, feelings dulled. "I just can't believe it" is a common response. Dreams at this stage may reflect this shock. A number of my clients have dreamed about loved ones being simultaneously alive and dead, reflecting their confusion. For example, Tamara dreamed that her husband was dead on the bed when suddenly the living husband walked into the room. She felt torn between the dead and the living husband. Which should she relate to? Which was real?

Others dream about their loved one's being dead and awaken with the hope that it was all just a bad dream. Or a person may appear vital and healthy in a dream, convincing the dreamer that "He's alive after all! He didn't die." These dreams reflect the shock and denial that predominate throughout this early stage, when a person is struggling to integrate this new information into his or her reality. Shock and denial help to buffer a person from the full impact of the loss, and dreams during this period may perform the same function.

On the other hand, many people in this early stage of grieving do not dream of the deceased at all. Instead, they find themselves searching in their dreams for the person without success. In *Mourning Unlived Lives*, Judith Savage states that searching dreams mostly occur shortly after the death itself and that they often stop when the griever begins to accept the reality of the loss.

Eventually, though, the fact of death hits hard, eliciting powerful and often overwhelming waves of emotions. When this happens, chaotic dreams with dark, even frightening images are common. In this period, many people dream that they are lost or confused, or they may dream about being swept up in some tidal wave or storm. It helps to understand that these dreams reflect what is taking place in the psyche: a breaking down of old structures and the welling up of primal emotions, both of which can contribute to a sense of being out of control. The loss of a loved one shakes up the very foundation of your life, flooding you with such intense feelings that normal functioning seems impossible. The resulting disorientation can be debilitating, but it can also shatter your limited sense of yourself. If you can surrender to this process of breaking down and dissolving, grief will transform you. You will emerge from it stronger and more vital than you were when you entered it.

Elva, who lost her father in her college years, had repeated dreams of being lost on dark streets and searching through dark houses. After her father's death, she felt utterly lost and depressed. She told me that her dreams comforted her by reflecting so accurately in images what she was experiencing emotionally. They also guided her quite explicitly toward the inner work that she needed to do in her grief. In one dream, she asked a man if she could explore his house, for she had heard that it had many secret passageways. After a long silence, the man told her that she had her own house now. Elva argued with him. "But I want to explore your house because of its secret passages." "Your house has secret passages, too," came the reply. "No, it doesn't," insisted Elva. "Yes, the secret passages are there." "Where?" "In the closets." "But I've looked in all the closets." "The passages are there. You have to clean out the closets first."

Elva realized that if she cleaned out her psychic closets, discarding what she could no longer use, she would have access to something new. She was excited about where the

secret passages might lead. Alongside the dark images in her
dreams there were whispers of confirmation that she was
progressing through her grief and not just stuck in her depression, as she had feared.

During the first year after my own father's death, I had
a series of dreams that my house was being remodeled, room
by room. Starting with the foundation, each room had to be
torn apart in order to be rebuilt. It was hard for me to visualize the outcome in the midst of this remodeling, that the
violent tearing down of walls and breaking of windows could
ultimately create a more spacious and livable room. Indeed,
my father's death did tear apart the world I had known and,
as I shared my grief with friends and family, many walls came
down, generating more vulnerability and intimacy in my relationships.

One of the dangers during deep grief is that the person
will hold on to grief, even when the psyche is ready to let it
end. Although it is more likely for people to wrench themselves prematurely out of their grief, some do hold onto it
and refuse to reenter the arena of daily life. If this goes on
for too long, it is not uncommon for a deceased loved one
to appear in dreams and encourage or admonish the dreamer
to go on with life. After his mother's death, a man wrote me
that his deceased brother appeared to him in a dream and
told him, "It is not your time yet, so live. But when it is time,
bring a sweater, for it's cold."

Throughout the long, active phase of grief, dreams about
the deceased loved one are reassuring. These dreams demonstrate that an ongoing relationship exists, even though it
is common during this time to doubt this. Ronald had a
dream about his wife, Linda, six months after she died. Since
he had not dreamed about her since her death, he was overjoyed to see her. As they talked and visited, he told her that
he had doubted that the relationship with her would continue after her death. He thought that she would no longer
be involved with him or his life. Linda was angry to hear

that he had had so little faith and lovingly chastised him. In the dream, he realized that without a doubt she was present within him.

Dreams can sometimes take you through a loved one's dying, even years after the event. Most often, such dreams occur late in the grieving process, but in fact they can occur at any time. If you do find yourself reliving a loved one's death in your dreams, and if you find these episodes disturbing and/or repetitive, it can be useful to perform exercise 3, Imagining a Loved One's Passing, in chapter 2.

Dreams often change in content as we move out of grief and into acceptance of the death, challenging us to live with a greater sense of aliveness and authenticity. Changes in self-concept, values, career and work, relationships, and religious and spiritual beliefs that have been developing below the surface throughout grief now begin to manifest outwardly. This is a time ripe with ideas, creativity, and potential, a time of expansion, stretching, and thinking big. Dreams at this stage suggest new possibilities, directions, and hopes. They thus reflect excitement about coming changes as well as any resistance, hesitation, and doubts that may surface in response. Elva, who had dreamed about the dark streets for so many months, experienced a change in her dreams in the weeks leading up to the first anniversary of her father's death. In one dream, a small coffin sat on the altar in a church. On the coffin was written, "A new life is born today." She also dreamed that she was being married in a Hindu ceremony. Elva attributed this dream to changes in her self-esteem that she had experienced since her father's death. She felt much more loving and accepting of herself and more confident in her capacity to confront challenging situations. Again, close to the first anniversary of her parent's death, another client dreamed that she was climbing a tall ladder and, just as she reached the top rungs of the ladder, was helped over the top by a woman who gave her a boost from behind.

Often, dreams at the end of grief reflect changes in the inner relationship with a deceased loved one. By this time, you might be trusting that the relationship will continue and no longer will need to be confirmed through repeated dreams, as was necessary earlier. You may come to expect long periods in which a loved one does not appear in your dreams at all, but you could find yourself savoring occasional dream visits. More than a year after her father's death, a client had a dream in which she had a date with her father in a lovely old hotel. She dressed up, bought two glasses of wine (a full-bodied cabernet for her father, a rosy zinfandel for herself), and went downstairs to meet him. He was healthy and slim, as he had been in younger days. They were both overjoyed and toasted one another.

A moving dream that clearly demonstrates a beloved's dream visit in the emergence phase is described in Paul Ebbinger's book *Restless Mind, Quiet Thoughts*. Over a year after Paul's suicide, his father, who posthumously published Paul's journals, had a dream that he and his son were hiking together in the mountains. Walking along in silence for a time, his son appeared content and healthy. He then told his father, "Dad, all of my earlier confusion and despair has lifted. It's so much better for me here; I can see clearly that the world just wasn't really suited for me. Strange how we humans have drifted, generation after generation, further and further from any natural kind of life . . . If I could only have trusted my self—my insides—just a little more back then, I might have made it . . . Now, I'm going to take the steeper trail to the right, if you continue to the left, there's a great view just ahead up there. So my journey continues—and so does yours. We'll talk again the next time we meet. Until then, adios" (Ebbinger, p. 195). Paul and his father meet in this dream, as they would have in life. They share silence and words and then part, each taking a different path. There is the assumption that in time they will meet again—perhaps in a dream.

Thus, your dreams are precious gifts that will guide you

through the challenges of grief and remind you that in the imagination, you have not lost contact with those who have died. Your dreams will let you know if you are suppressing your grief and inform you of what you need to attend to in order to heal. They will change in response to shifts in your grieving. Initial dreams often reflect the shock and denial that the griever is experiencing; dreams throughout the most active phase of grief may be chaotic, even frightening. After many months of intense grieving, your dreams may encourage you to expand, engage in new possibilities, and explore new directions. Trust the wisdom of your dreams; they connect you to the vast, imaginative realm of the unconscious where resources for deepening and healing from loss abound. The following steps will help you retrieve and work with your dreams.

SEVEN STEPS FOR WORKING WITH DREAMS

1. The first step is to establish a relationship with your dreams as messengers from the unconscious. Perhaps you have always ignored your dreams or devalued the messages from this part of your psyche. But most cultures of the world have used dreams as healing tools, and Freud and Jung, the great genius/explorers in the mapping of the human psyche, proved the great value dreams have for us as conduits to instinct, buried memories, and the unconscious. If you have avoided this area of your reality, you may have to convince the unconscious that you do value its feedback and that now you are willing to listen. If you approach dreams with respect, humility, and receptivity, you will build a constructive relationship with your unconscious.

2. Before you go to sleep, actively decide that you want to remember a dream, that you are open to whatever the

unconscious presents to you. If you are currently struggling with a particular problem or issue, ask for a dream that will address it specifically.

Put a pen and paper (or tape recorder) and a flashlight by your bed, and make the commitment to write down whatever fragment or dream that you remember. Then go to sleep. If you awaken in the middle of the night with a dream, write it down immediately. Make brief notes that you can elaborate on later. Many assume that they will remember a dream, only to find that it has flown the next day.

In the morning, don't get out of bed or talk to anyone until you have taken some time to reflect on your dreams. Without editing, write down whatever you remember, including fragments. Sometimes a fragment is like the tail of a fish. If you take hold of it firmly, the rest of the dream may follow out of the watery depths. Even if you don't remember the rest of the dream, the fragment itself can often be a rich source of insights.

If you have trouble remembering your dreams, be patient. Don't give up. Some friends and clients have had success with writing on paper or even in the air: "I want to remember a dream tonight." Or you can work with a guided imagery exercise in which you close your eyes, imagine yourself going to sleep and having a dream, and then awakening in the morning with a clear memory of the dream.

3. Later, record your dream in a dream journal. Referring to your notes, write the dream in the present tense as though it were unfolding now. Then, give it a title. Writing the dream down in a special place gives it importance and sends the message to the unconscious that you are taking its messages seriously.

After you have recorded your dream, take some time to reflect on it. Prepare for the unexpected; admit your ignorance. Approach the dream humbly, setting aside

snap judgments. Remember that a dream works on many
levels at once; a dream can never be reduced to just one
meaning. You may feel baffled, disturbed, and even resistant. All this is natural in working with dreams. Your
task at this point is simply to just sit with the dream images and let them work on you. After a lifetime of studying dreams, Carl Jung confessed that they remained a
mystery to him. He did not feel confident that his way of
working with dreams could be called a method. However,
Jung did feel certain that something always came of med-
itating on a dream, turning it over and over for a period
of time.

4. To begin exploring what needs resolution in a dream, ask
   questions of the dream and of the dream figures. Here
   are some sample questions to pose:

   - What am I doing or not doing in the dream?
   - What are the significant actions in this dream?
   - What are the feelings in this dream?
   - Who are the dream figures in this dream?
   - What are the issues, conflicts, and unresolved situa-
     tions?
   - What possibilities for healing are present?
   - What questions does this dream raise for me?
   - What images stand out?
   - What associations come up for me with each image?
   - What is being wounded and/or healed in the dream?
   - Does this dream have a relationship to other dreams?
   - Do any situations in my daily life come to mind as I
     reflect on this dream?
   - What new choices does this dream suggest or inspire?

   Here are some sample questions to ask of the people
   who appear in your dream:

   - What do you want?
   - What do you want to show me?

- Do you have any messages for me?
- What is your gift?
- What do I need to do to develop a relationship with you?
- Where do you want to take me?

5. Look for threads connecting this dream with other dreams. If you find yourself dreaming regularly about a similar theme, in your dream journal, read carefully over all the dreams in that series. Perhaps an early dream in a series introduces the issues to be explored in subsequent dreams. Or maybe a later dream offers critical information that was missing in earlier ones.

6. As you move through these steps, remember that a dream can never be reduced to just one meaning. If you feel confident about any one interpretation of a dream, stay open to other possibilities as well. Writer/psychologist James Hillman insightfully writes, "If we think back on any dream that has been important to us, as time passes and the more we reflect on it, the more we discover in it, and the more varied the directions that lead out of it. Whatever certainty it once might have given shifts into complexities beyond clear formulations each time the dream is studied anew. The depth of even the simplest image is truly fathomless. This unending, embracing depth is one way dreams show their love" (Hillman, p. 200).

7. Other methods will help you explore your dream further:

- Dialogue with dream figures or images.
- Adopt the persona of the different people, animals, or objects in your dream and reexperience the dream from that perspective.
- Paint or draw the dream; sculpt a dream image.
- Act out your dreams.
- In your imagination, go back into the dream and re-

dream it. The following exercise will show you how to reenter your dream.

Reentering a Dream

When you have a dream about one who has died, write it down. Take a few minutes to recall the most significant or vivid part of the dream in which this person appeared. Then, close your eyes and reenter the dream by placing yourself in that environment. Even if you didn't notice any smells, sounds, or textures in your original dream, experience this place now with all your senses. Look around you. Touch, smell, listen. Continue to explore this environment with your senses until you feel fully present in your body. This will help you move from your memory of the dream to experience it in the present.

Next, pay close attention to the person's expression, movements, and dress. If the details seem vague, focus, as you might through the lens of a camera, on one small part of that person. As you concentrate on this part, other details may become clearer. Then expand your focus to include the whole person.

It takes time to develop your inner senses; you may not be able to see images clearly the first few times you work with imagery exercises. Even without gleaning any details of the person, you'll be able to sense his or her presence. Be aware of what you are feeling.

To create an opportunity for interaction, approach the person directly. You may want to ask the questions cited above as possible queries of your dream figures.

In the following days, look for ways in which you can express the dream images you created when you were asleep. For example, a client who had a powerful dream about a lion felt inspired to buy a shirt with a lion's head painted on it. Wearing this shirt brought out the lion in him; it actually made him feel more courageous and energetic. In this way, a dream is a call to wake up and live more fully.

Chapter 4

Letters: Beginning a Correspondence

Dreams of deceased loved ones surprise and comfort us. Most people feel such dreams occur too infrequently and are deeply frustrated to lose the connection upon awakening, as if a phone line had suddenly gone dead. They wait and wait for more dreams, believing them to offer the only way to make contact. But you don't have to wait. Use the communication methods in this and succeeding chapters to gain access to and explore this unique relationship. You can do the exercises in the order they are presented or simply try the ones you feel most drawn to. Always retreat to the sanctuary you have established in your home to perform the activity you choose.

WRITING A LETTER

We begin with a technique for opening a communication that is perhaps the easiest approach, affording the least resistance, even when both parties are living. Writing a letter allows you to reflect, choose, rework, revise, and take as much time as you need to express yourself fully.

Within the terrain of a letter, you have the freedom to express yourself honestly, directly, and completely without worrying about the other person's response. This sort of carte blanche will help you express whatever you have held back or silenced in your communication and will thus pin-point the issues you need to resolve in your relationship. For example, write about what experiences you have been through since your loved one died, what you miss, what you have learned about yourself and the relationship, what you appreciate and resent in your relationship, what you want to carry on. If certain issues have surfaced since the death, or issues have begun to bother you that were never addressed when the person was alive, write about these. If you are bringing up an event from the past that you wish to resolve, you may want to redefine what happened, de-scribing exactly how you felt about it and how you'd like to change it. This event has affected you and what you want for the present. Remember, you'll find that your commu-nication flows more freely if you avoid blaming, preaching, or demanding. Still, express yourself honestly and authen-tically, not avoiding or dampening your real feelings, even if they are distressingly negative.

Don't feel discouraged if your first letter is full of anger. It is common to feel angry at your loved one for dying and for causing the hurts and disappointments that people always do effect upon each other to one degree or another. You may need to express uncomfortable feelings, thoughts, and memories before you can move on to feeling more compas-sionate, loving, or understanding. It may not be possible to make this shift in one letter; it may take several letters to get to a point of closure. But remember throughout the pro-cess that as soon as you start writing a letter to your loved one, you are initiating a healing that will go at its own pace. You can actively participate in this process, but you can't control or force it.

Here are some sample questions you might ask yourself as you write your letter:

- What experiences have I been through since my loved one's death?
- What do I miss?
- What do I regret?
- What issues in our relationship remain unresolved?
- What do I resent?
- What do I appreciate?
- What have I learned about myself, my loved one, and my relationship?
- What do I want to carry on?

Ask yourself the following questions after you have written your letter:

- Was I open and honest?
- Did I express my love and appreciation?
- Did I address unresolved issues in our relationship?
- Do I still feel regrets?
- Are any resentments still bothering me?
- Is anything left unsaid?
- Do I feel forgiveness? Do I feel more understanding?

MARIANNE'S LETTER

Marianne wrote this letter to her brother, who had died in an accident while he was attending college in England:

DEAREST JAMES,

I ask where you are and in the voices of the rain and the wind I sense you telling me that this is the wrong question, that you *are* but there is no *where*. It's a tentative question I've asked. I realize that I'm resisting talking to you. I don't want to open myself up to the pain again. My throat feels tight and my neck and shoulders are very still. They are capping off my heart's feelings.

I've tried several ways of reaching out to you, but there is no clear imagery, no sound of your voice. It's even hard for me to see your face. What does come up is a stream of pictures, like watching cuts of home movies out of our life together as we grew up. There seems to be no way to stop the stream to look at a single "frame." Our brief life together flows by and disappears—such a brief moment. If only I could wind it back and show you how precious you were to me.

Now the tears come . . . those "if onlys" cause such pain.

I realize how little I have allowed myself to feel my own sorrow in your death. Mum and Dad were so overwhelmed and in such agony that I felt I had to be there for them, to support them. There didn't seem to be anywhere for me to go to grieve for myself. No one in the States knew you, and Mum and Dad actually asked me not to come home for your funeral because they didn't want to add to the pain by having to say good-bye to me afterwards. I didn't know any better then. I didn't have enough self-confidence to override them and do what my heart told me: to go home, to be with them and with you, to see your poor body, to hear the words and songs of your funeral, to cry with Mum and Dad holding your ashes in a little box on my lap, to be in the silence of the mourning house.

One of the hardest things for me is to move beyond the stuckness I feel about what actually happened to you. I know that it was early morning; you were on your way to work. Your van had broken down and you were trying to fix it. Some other people had stopped and, I suppose, were going to try and help you. Then a lorry came by, too fast I imagine, and hit you, and drove on. It's possible that the driver never knew what he had done. I know they never found him; that felt so unfinished for so long.

The other people saw him hit you. At first I tried to imagine the scene over and over again. It's almost as if I was trying to force the reality into my own body so that I could realize what had happened. There are so many unanswered questions: Did you die instantly? What happened to your body? Was it badly damaged? Was there a lot of pain? And in the death itself: Were you free to go or were you caught not knowing whether you were alive or dead?

I know that you were with Mum, for she felt and heard you reassuring her. That helped us all, I think. There's so much that I don't know and still don't feel able to talk about with Mum and Dad. Maybe I don't need to. This is something for me to explore in myself. I need to see if I can just let go or if I have to actually re-create what happened as a way to bring closure.

So, now, after all these years, what do I write to you? I don't even remember the date of your death. October 10th, I think, 1980. The year that Mount St. Helens exploded. I remember those endless pictures of gray smoke. It was a gray fall, a gray winter. It's hard to pierce through the fog with which I shroud that time.

Sometimes I see you very vividly in my dreams. It feels as if your death was the real dream and that, when I wake up, I can just call you on the phone and we'll be talking and laughing as though no time has passed since we last saw each other.

How little time we really spent together after we both went to boarding school and then to college—our culture didn't really invite passion, did it? Nonetheless, I treasure the sweet, loving connection that we made the last few times we saw each other, and I know in my heart that you also cared and loved intensely. My heart still feels pain, not to be able to hold you and express that love through physical presence.

I do believe you are with me in some way. I sometimes think that I can feel you encouraging me as I make all these changes in my life—going to school, creating my wonderful relationship with G., waking up to life in ways that encourage me to move over edges into new places.

Taking this class and writing this letter have pushed me to really pay attention to the sense of your presence. As I write this, I can feel a little shift as if I'm releasing my grip on the pain of the memories and allowing myself to make some space for a new relationship to you. A little panic comes up. "But I don't want to forget. The pain helps me remember." And the answer comes: "Let go of the old pain. It prevents you from opening to your deepest creative feelings. There will be sadness and tears, but the passion can only grow if you allow the light to come in. Release your grip. Let go."

James, be with me in my letting go of you. Maybe this sounds a bit crazy, but I know that I'll feel your presence in life more clearly if I release my fear of losing you. I have lost you in the physical realm. You've gone. But I'm beginning to realize the truth of other sorts of presence—in energy, awareness, intensity. I know you're there.

Now, a few days later, I look back over some of what I've written. The first thing that comes up is a kind of wonder at how deeply I still feel love for you. It's so alive, so present. With that feeling comes a little shyness. I know there is so much that I will never learn about you and your life. I know that your friends from Oxford were much closer to you as an adult than I ever was, and there's a part of me that feels almost presumptuous about my sense of intimacy and love.

So much has changed in our family since your death, I think *because* of your death. We are close and attentive now. We treasure our times together and talk from the heart about many things. We are much more loving—openly loving. What a price to pay in order to claim and express our love for each other. And what a commitment, because of that price, to really honor our connection from the heart. In a way, it is the "you" in us which energizes our love for each other.

I'm reluctant to stop writing as if, by doing so, I'll break this feeling of connection with you. But I know now that I can do this. I know that the pain is bearable and that by opening, it lightens and releases you, and me.

So thank you for being with me. Thank you for your loving soul.

Like so many who have written letters to deceased loved ones, Marianne experienced significant shifts in her grief as she wrote her letter. At first, she felt hesitant to begin writing, because she knew doing so would open her up to pain again. As she made the commitment to proceed and memories surfaced—memories of her brother, their relationship, and his death—she realized that the unanswered questions about his death had impeded her recovery from grief. It is common for people who were not present at a loved one's accidental death to obsess over possible scenarios. I often suggest that clients work with active imagination exercises, such as Internal Communication with the Dying in chapter 2, in order to participate in the passing and say good-bye. As Marianne explored what could have happened the day her brother was killed, she opened to her pain, her grief began to flow, and her heart itself opened. Only then was she able to experience her deep love for James. She realized how much she still felt his presence in her life—"in energy, awareness, intensity." And at this point in the letter, Marianne felt a shift occurring: the release of her painful memories made room for a new relationship with James. Instead of obsessing on her loss, she now saw the positive changes that had occurred because of his death; for example, the family's becoming closer and more open with one another.

Marianne's connection with James, which she was unable to feel at the beginning of the letter, was so strong at the end of the letter that she actually found it difficult to stop writing. She knew she could now bear the pain, experience it, and let it go. She also found that she could have a new relationship with her brother, one that was full of love and appreciation. In writing this letter, Marianne felt, she had released both James and herself.

Henri Nouwen wrote about his mother in *In Memoriam*: "In these weeks of mourning she died in me more and more every day, making it impossible for me to cling to her as my mother. Yet by letting her go I did not lose her. Rather, I found that she is closer to me than ever" (Nouwen, p. 60).

AMY'S LETTER TO HER FATHER

Amy, a workshop participant, wrote to her father, who had died eight years before. After starting her letter several times, she realized that she was avoiding the more difficult aspects of the relationship. Once she brought her resentments and regrets out into the open, the letter began to flow.

DEAR DAD,

So much has happened in my life since you died (and how often, for the first year or so, I had the thought, "Gee, I'll have to call Dad and tell him!"). Although you might not understand some of what I'm up to these days, I'm sure you would be pleased to know how much I've grown, and that I'm finally on a path of my own choosing and for which I have great enthusiasm.

But first, let me talk a little about when you died. I am really grateful to have spent those last few months with you. We got to know one another in ways we never had before. I felt as if you were actually proud of me, that you finally were able to see me at work. You saw me as responsible, competent, and as smart as you always thought I was! I was able to see you much mellower than you'd been when I was growing up. You were gentler, more loving, more accepting, easier to be with. And I really enjoyed being with you, the times we had the chance. I loved finding out how much we actually agreed on, after all those years of fighting one another. It made me feel good to see how pleased you were about me and how I "turned out."

I've started parts of this letter several times. I realize that I am hesitant to recount everything. However, I want to say what's so for me right now and I want to be as honest with you as I am with other people—honest without blame or guilt. So much has passed between us, so much anger, hurt, and confusion. What I feel right now is forgiveness—for you and for myself. From that place there's nothing to do except just be with you and realize how much I love you and you love me.

As much as I adore Mommy and feel connected to her, I am realizing that YOU have had more influence on me than anyone . . . much more than I ever realized until just now. Whether I was rebelling or trying to win your approval (which seemed impossible to me as a child), whether I was emulating you and learning the many useful things you taught me, or rejecting you as a model, or trying to hurt you or whatever . . . you were the seed around which Amy formed. I think that, since you went away, I've unraveled the layers and have finally found the essence of me. It's almost as if I can recreate myself now in my relationship with you, rather than bounce off you in reaction.

I think it's probably very simple: you always loved me and didn't even think to tell me or reassure me of that—it's where you came from.

Do I have some regrets? Yes. I regret the things I did to hurt you. I regret I didn't kiss you good-bye that last night. I was afraid I'd wake you up and you'd have another seizure, but I wish I'd done it. And I wish I'd come to see your body after you had died. I don't know why . . . it was one of those things I thought about doing and talked myself out of. I try not to talk myself out of things that I feel like doing anymore.

Do I have some resentments? Yes. I resent that, because of whatever pressures you were experiencing and maybe because you didn't get much unconditional love as a kid, you were really hard on me. You always reminded me of my potential by letting me know that I wasn't fulfilling it; you often disapproved of me; you called me a "mixed-up little girl" when what I really needed was some understanding; you hit me way too much; you were rough with me when I needed tenderness; you had no respect for my feelings; you criticized me; you tried to scare me about sex rather than educate me, and you left me terribly vulnerable to the very things you were hoping to protect me from; you never told me I was pretty. It took me a long time to work through feelings of shame and to find my own self-esteem again, Dad. But I have, and I will not spend the rest of my life blaming you or myself. I'm hesitant to say that I forgive you, because it sounds so ungrateful for all you did for me. I finally realized they're not connected. You did what you did for me, and you did some things that really hurt me and which I took very personally and seriously. I thank you for what you did do for me and I forgive you for what you did that wasn't loving. I forgive myself, too, and hope that you forgive me as well.

Now that the hard and ugly stuff is out in the open, maybe I could just say what I love about you and what I wish, okay? You were very handsome, Daddy, and you had a great body for a long time! So many people loved you. You worked hard and made sure we had plenty to eat and clothes to wear. I know you loved us and you loved Mommy, and you expressed it the best you could. You took care of your brother, and your mother, and even people who worked for you. You probably did many things for people that you never told anyone about. In many ways, you were a very generous man. I wish I'd been enough of my own person to have talked with you more as a friend. Would you have talked more about personal things? Would you have shared what happened in the war or would you have always kept that to yourself, like Grandma still does? Is there anything you ever wanted to tell me that you didn't say? Would you tell me now?

Did you know that when you died, they put the flag at half-mast on the common? That was incredible. You did so much for that little town. You built your business from nothing to something great and you left Mom financially secure. Thank you for all those things, Dad.

I want to ask you something. Sometimes I remember what it felt like to be a very little girl, and at those times what I want is to be held by my Daddy, to be told that I'm beautiful and wonderful just the way I am and to hear you tell me you love me. Would it be okay if we did that once in a while? You don't have to say anything, just hold me, and I'll know. And you'll know that I love you, too, okay? Thanks, Daddy. I love you. And I miss you.

Amy had begun her letter by updating her father on her life. She then recalled her final months with him and expressed her appreciation for the time they had together. At this point, Amy admitted that she had other feelings toward her father as well, ones that were harder to express. She made a commitment to be honest with her father without blaming him. Through the powerful statement, "You were the seed around which Amy was formed," Amy acknowledged that her father had had a greater influence on her than anyone else and that, as a result, his criticisms and his withholding of expressions of love had had a devastating impact on her self-esteem. Once Amy communicated her regrets and resentments, she felt ready to forgive both her father and herself. Only then could she acknowledge all the positive ways he had impacted her life, the family, and their community. By the end of the letter, Amy felt so close to her father that she asked him to hold her as her Daddy from time to time. So many adults who have lost a parent have said to me, "I just want my Mommy! I just want my Daddy!"

CHARLOTTE'S LETTER

The death of Charlotte's first friend had a deep impact on her life: she was eighteen years old when he died, and she vowed never to love again. Feeling guilty that her life would go on after her friend's had ended, she put aside her dreams for her future. By the time she wrote this letter, she had emerged from "thirteen years of darkness" and was able to express both how devastating her loss had been and how much the friendship had meant to her.

DEAR DONNIE,

Did I ever tell you about Howdy Doody? My family was living in Texas; I think I was about seven years old. As you know, my mother, like her mother before her, would not allow me to play with other children. Consequently, I was a lonely child. Howdy Doody was my friend. Then one day my mother shattered this love by telling me that he was not a real boy; he was a puppet who moved with strings attached to a stick that a man was controlling behind a curtain. My only friend wasn't real. I was crushed.

We met a few months later. They tell me that you gave me flowers from the garden. I cannot remember that incident, but I can remember the joy of being with you. My very own friend! You liked me and thought that I was lovable. It was the first time that I could be in a masculine presence without fear of being hit. My skinny legs were bare from under my little girl's skirt. There was no shame. I was free to be with you. I can remember my smile. It started from you to my depths, my soul, then to my heart, and then back to you again. Did you feel the same way? Were the flowers a deep red, and was the color of the stems and leaves a deep, dark green?

We were eighteen when you died, and I vowed never to love again. The great effect this vow would have on my life I could not have known. The pain of losing you was so immense. The guilt of getting over this pain was equally unbearable. There was no help for me; besides, I was probably too weak and emotionally undeveloped to receive it. My solution was to shut down. No more loving and risks, no more guilt, and no more grief. I call that period my thirteen years of darkness.

Were you there when I had the vision? I saw you sitting

with your one leg propped up beneath your chin, just as you used to. Then I revisited the cancer's pain and for the first time felt a huge fear. Were you as terrified of this pain as I was? I became nauseous. You looked so terrible, your growing adolescent body had withered into something grotesque. But how could I respond to this while caring for you? It took that long for me to feel the pain, the fear, and the devastation that death did to you. It has taken much longer to know how that devastation affected my life.

The next part of the vision was numinous. Your body metamorphosed into otherworldly colors of bright green and yellow. It slowly became an embryo. So beautiful! This vision was a wonderful gift. From then on, I knew that there was an afterlife.

Last May, I was cleaning house and listening to Joan Baez and Leonard Cohen. One of my favorite songs speaks of seeing one's true love. When I heard the last line, "And death had put an end to his growing," I was standing near a big chair. Suddenly, I leaned down on the chair, my heart pierced with the grief of losing you. From within, these words came: "I did not even know." You were my first love, and, until then, I had not known. My parents never allowed me to know what was important to me. Recently I have begun to know who I am and what I feel and need. These "knowings" have reminded me of my grief and how much I still miss you.

I'm in school now. A few weeks ago, I had a dream about you. I was telling you that I was going to get a Ph.D. Then I felt such tremendous guilt. Remember that last summer, when we all spent a day at a little lake? Sharon, you, and I were sitting and talking. Sharon had just shared her dreams for the future. There I was, with kids my own age. I expressed my desire to finish college. You said, "I just want to live," and then you swam away from us. It felt so bad. Have you forgiven me? How could I be so insensitive? My guilt banished me from the hopes of making something of myself. How could I ask for the prestige of an education when you had been denied life?

Now, after all these years, I am getting a Ph.D. I guess it is time to forgive myself.

You were my hope for the future. You were my first friend. If it had not been for you, I do not think I could have found my husband. I still miss you and there are times when I am still angry that you are gone. Now you have begun to help me in my dreams. For this, I am grateful.

LOVE, LOTTIE

Writing this poignant letter helped Charlotte, after years of agonized grieving, build a new relationship with Donnie. Instead of feeling guilty for making something of herself, Charlotte could now proudly share her academic accomplishments with Donnie and accept his help in her dreams.

WRITING A RESPONSE

The person you write to will never read your letter, of course, and can never actually respond in kind. But the techniques of internal communication allow you to frame a response to your heartfelt correspondence by engaging your imagination and opening yourself to realities that had been suppressed.

Let's look at an example of both a letter to a loved one and the response that emerged in the writer's imagination. Like many women, Ray had had a distant relationship with her father. As a young girl, she had yearned for his approval and encouragement—in fact, for any outward expression of love. Later, as she sat hour after hour with her dying father in the hospital, she treasured their moments of intimacy. She stroked her father's head and held his hand; they cried and talked together. After his death, she grieved not only the loss of her father but also the loss of new opportunities for intimacy. More than a year after his death, Ray wrote about her sadness and disappointment in a compelling letter to her father:

Driving through the green hills to the hospital, I push back tears, telling myself it will be easier to meet death in the springtime, the natural world around me singing a glorious cantata to life. I tell myself, springtime will be enough to hold me while you go on, swept along in the Great Dance. "The sheep have begun lambing," I say, trying to bring some joy to your bedside. You clasp my hand tightly, your face more candid than I have ever seen it, and softly we let the tears flow, crying together for all the lambs you'll never see in the windy fields, all the springtimes that will come and go without you.

When I think of reaching out to you now, Daddy, my heart aches. My whole being becomes aching sadness. This room where I sit in California, half a world away from any place you ever knew, feels strangely empty. I close my eyes and see you, frail, vulnerable, stripped of your stern pride. Daddy, if only you could have been soft with me before death was staring you down. If only we could have cried together, now and then, about the simple, sad things that happen in life.

Now that there is absolutely nothing left to protect or hide, could we talk? Now that there is nothing you could possibly lose, could we be close and real? Daddy, even now I am waiting, as I always waited, for you to give me something of yourself.

I remember how at breakfast (Mummy long gone into her busy day), you'd sit across the table from me, staring over my head out the window, eating in silence. Daddy, why didn't you ever talk to me? Why was I so invisible, so irrelevant, so disappointing to you?

Did we get entangled in some mutual knot? I can't remember. Mostly, I only remember the pain. And the time I saw you cry. When Bess died in the bog at the edge of the pond. I know you loved that pony. But when I called from college: "Please, please bring her in this winter, Daddy. She is getting too old to winter outside." "Nonsense," you said. "She's fine." Why was it so hard for you to admit that animals, children, people need love?

In writing her father's response, Ray saw into her father's reasons for being neglectful and hurtful in their relationship as she had never seen before. In answer to her question, "Why was it so hard for you to admit that . . . people need love?" her father's response yielded these poignant words: *"Because"*, she wrote in his voice, *"then I'd have had to admit that I needed love. And what if I wasn't loved? What if no one loved me? That would have been too hard to bear."*

Ray immediately reacted with a question, and quite naturally an active dialogue developed between them.

RAY: Is that why you would say those cruel things to me whenever we were alone together in the car? "Nobody likes you," you'd say. Why did you say such hurtful things?

DAD: Because you were not the child I wanted. You were too wild, too emotional, naked to the world. I couldn't show you off. You had no polished front. You were too raw, too vulnerable. You made me hate you.

RAY: How?

DAD: You weren't happy enough.

RAY: Yes, I remember when I was about seven, you chiding me, "What's the matter with you? Why don't you glow like other kids?" I would sit for hours in my room, studying my face in the mirror, wondering why I didn't glow. Daddy, how could I glow for you? I didn't know how. Couldn't you see the light inside couldn't shine through the drowning sadness, the shame of never being enough, the ache for something I couldn't name? It was all I could do to walk the fine line, to dodge the blows, to be invisible enough to grow and leave home. Daddy, sometimes I won-

der, can you see me now, prying off this awful legacy,
becoming the person I never dared to dream I could
be?

Rereading her father's response several months later, it
became even clearer to Ray that her father had rejected her
because he couldn't tolerate his own emotional neediness.
Throughout his life, he had tried to pretend that normal
people don't need love; in spite of this, he became vulnerable, emotional, and raw as he was dying. Ray described him
in this state as "beautiful, sadly awkward, and tragically like
the child he had found so hard to love." Ray's correspondence with her father was a breakthrough in her relationship
with him. Asking her father hard and painful questions, she
elicited thoughtful, honest responses from him. By the end
of this first dialogue, she was developing compassion and
understanding for her father. Her final question, "Daddy,
sometimes I wonder, can you see me now, prying off this
awful legacy, becoming the person I never dared to dream
I could be?" created closure to this first dialogue but opened
up new topics for the next one. It seems that she now felt
ready for her father to get to know the woman she had become.

To write your own response, first make sure you have
truly stated your concerns in your own letter. Then, on a
separate paper and in a separate sanctuary session, compose
a response in the voice of the recipient. This can take the
form of a short reply, a letter, or a dialogue, a technique
covered in the following chapter. If you write a letter, address it to yourself and start writing without judging or editing. To free the imagination and foster empathy, you can
close your eyes and picture the person's face, while saying
your own name silently or out loud as the person would say
it. You can also focus on some particular favored phrase or
look closely at a photograph of the person. All of these may
help make the person feel more accessible to you as you

begin to write. After a few paragraphs, you may find, as others have, that the words flow and the letter expresses more of your family member's thoughts and feelings than your own. The imagination's capacity to put you simultaneously inside yourself and inside others may feel disconcerting and unnerving but also liberating. When you have finished this letter, reread it, opening yourself to its contents.

Chapter 5

Dialogues: Going Where They Take You

Writing a dialogue with your loved one can take you deeper and into more unexpected, unknown places once you've opened communication with a letter, or letters, and a response. This technique is especially effective when the initial correspondence has turned up particular issues you want to explore.

Initiate your dialogue by identifying the issue or concern as sensitively as you can and then expressing your feelings about it—all this on paper following your name. Then write the other person's name and open your imagination to his or her responsive words. If there is no reaction, you can ask questions to help the dialogue begin. Let the dialogue unfold spontaneously; don't interfere or control it. Be open to the unexpected and to new information and ways of relating.

Look to the things that your loved one passed on to you or to activities that you shared together to invoke the presence of the other person. For example, Caron feels her grandmother's presence every time she bakes pies, since her grandmother had taught her to bake as a child. Attending my niece's ordination as a deacon in the Episcopal Church, I was reciting the Nicene Creed with the rest of the congregation when I clearly heard my father's voice beside me. In the same steady, reassuring manner he had when we had attended church together throughout my childhood, he was saying the prayer along with me. Feeling such a sense of your loved one's presence will help you become open to explore dialogue, whether aloud or silently.

As is usually the case with internal communication, the amount of time that has passed since the death has little impact on the effectiveness of the method. Almost ten years after her father's death, Sophie wrote a dialogue between herself and her father, William. In the last years of his life, a series of ministrokes had severely restricted William's movement and impaired his vision. Her mother, Karen, had devotedly nursed him for three years in their apartment, but eventually, she collapsed with exhaustion. Sophie then convinced her mother to put William in a nursing home, where he died ten days later. The night before his death, Sophie visited William and, even though he seemed comatose, she spoke to him. In an emotional breakthrough, she told him, "I love you." When a nurse called Sophie the next day with the news of his death, she felt numb yet relieved that William was no longer suffering. After arranging for the cremation, she stoically went on with her life. It wasn't until years later that she realized how much she still held him in her heart and mind, quoting him to friends and treasuring the books he had loved. In her living room stands a cherry bookcase with leaded glass doors that holds his favorite books. Sometimes Sophie imagines that her father's spirit lives behind the tattered books in that bookcase. She writes, "Today his spirit is more alive for me than in those last months of life. So it is with fear and hope that I try to engage in a conversation with Dad." Looking at an old photo of William, she began her dialogue with a question. Immediately, she received a response, and from that point on, the dialogue seemed almost to write itself.

SOPHIE: Dad, are you here with me? I have an old photo taken after my graduation. Your handsome face is beaming and you are standing so tall.

DAD: Little Doe, Baby Doe.

SOPHIE: You *are* here! I have sensed it. I have felt your presence lately. Can we talk, I mean *really* talk? Sometimes I feel that you hide behind your wit. I miss your wit, but I prefer that we talk honestly. Just talk and be yourself with me. I want you to know that I love you.

DAD: I do love you. I guess I never said it in just so many words. Words: what hollow, inarticulate struggle this mess of verbiage!

SOPHIE: Can we go back nine-plus years when you were living out your last days?

DAD: Why? I was on the rack; a time of torture. You rarely visited me. "How sharper than a serpent's tooth is an ungrateful child" [a quote from *King Lear*].

SOPHIE: Yes, I was afraid and overwhelmed. I felt helpless.

DAD: Well, it's water under the bridge. I have been released from that body, released from that vale of tears and suffering. . . .

SOPHIE: We can't change the past. I guess I need to focus on my life now. But I wish that you and I could connect on a regular basis. Can we continue this dialogue?

DAD: Sure, I have all the time in the world. But you! Get on the stick, kid!

SOPHIE: I need to ask you: Is there anything you feel like saying to me that you were not able to say when you were alive?

DAD: Baby Doe, I do love you. I loved you then, I love you now. In spite of the bad times and the drinking. I wish I could have been more direct and said it then and showed it then.

SOPHIE: Did *I* ever share my feelings with you? We both seemed to hide behind our wit. I don't want to hide anymore. I simply say to you that I love you and I miss you and I feel that you live on in my memory. I want to take time out to acknowledge these feelings. Starting right now . . .

DAD: Just don't be obsessed. Next thing, you'll be doing automatic writing and holding séances—hokum! Remember me, but live your life! Seek out joy, not tragedy. Hold the phone; let's connect again—later.

SOPHIE: Dear old Dad! Thank you for your gifts. Until we connect again . . .

In this dialogue, the father's unique style of communicating comes through very clearly. Sophie hadn't expected this, nor had she anticipated that the dialogue would flow so easily. She was delighted that she had finally broken through to such a deep and honest level of interaction with her father. She had expressed her love to him, and his direct expression of love moved her profoundly.

The healing that Sophie experienced in writing this piece radiated out to her relationship with her mother, too. Her mother, Karen, called Sophie soon afterward, asking her for some time to talk about dying, a subject that Karen had been avoiding. This development surprised and delighted Sophie, but was really part of the larger process. As I will discuss in part III, bringing the light of imagination to bear on a suppressed family issue in a dialogue with a deceased person often clears away barriers in communication with living family members.

On her deceased grandmother's birthday, Stephanie wrote a dialogue with her, the grandparent to whom she felt closest. When her grandmother told her in her last years that she had lived a long life and was ready to die, Stephanie joked that her grandmother had to see her married first. Her grandmother died just a few months after Stephanie was engaged. Stephanie later moved into her grandmother's house and, four years after her death, was still living there when she wrote this dialogue.

STEPHANIE: Gramma, there's something I've always wondered about. Were you happy with your life? Growing up, it always seemed so normal to me.

GRAMMA: It was the simple things in life that gave me the greatest joy: the flowers in the garden, a clean house. I enjoyed the daily routine of my life.

STEPHANIE: But didn't you want more?

GRAMMA: By the time you knew me, Steph, I was past middle age. Don't forget that in my younger days, I had worked and taught in a one-room schoolhouse. I had done some traveling. I had married and raised two children and had already lost my husband. I had also seen many changes in the name of progress in the world. So, yes, at one point, I wanted more, but then there came a time to realize what I had and to commit to that. I have been very lucky to have been close to my brothers and sisters and to have had a son and daughter and then grandchildren. This was my life. Stephanie, I wish the same for you. I worry about you sometimes. Don't let the wild spirit in you blind you to the simple joys around you. Life is already here; don't run away from it. Listen to it and live it.

STEPHANIE: I miss you, Gramma. I miss your stories. You were the connection to my past and my history. I'm sorry I didn't listen more carefully or write it all down.

GRAMMA: We all have those regrets. What you need is in your heart. You know the basics. I probably had too many stories! Do you have a sense of your family tree, something that connects you back in time? That's what's important. Remember that you and your sisters, brother, and cousins are the living foliage—the leaves of the tree today. One day, you, too, will fall to the earth to make room for the next generation. In the meantime, take the life that has flowed through this tree to you and make it your own. I am proud of you already and know that if you remain connected, good things will come.

STEPHANIE: Gramma, I feel like I'm not really able to say anything. This is not what I expected to happen, though I really didn't know *what* to expect.

GRAMMA: I never got the chance to say good-bye to you, either. These are a few things I would have liked to have said, but probably you weren't ready to hear them.

STEPHANIE: Does this mean you're leaving me? Maybe I shouldn't have done this. You had a message for me all along. You are much stronger than I gave you credit for.

GRAMMA: Steph, I am not the same, obviously, as you remember me. What I said to you is important. I needed to tell you those things. We have a connection, you and I, which can't be broken; but, yes, my purpose is finished here. I have been waiting and knew you would come back to hear it.

STEPHANIE: [I no longer sense her presence in the house as I have since I've lived there. She is gone.] Gramma, don't go! [I start crying.]

At first, Stephanie felt panic at no longer sensing her grandmother's presence; she had not intended to break the connection. Furthermore, the dialogue had yielded up very different answers than Stephanie had expected. However, Stephanie felt comforted that her grandmother, having delivered her message, was finally free to move on. In letting go of Gramma, Stephanie felt her own freedom, a freedom that was both exciting and frightening. She realized that it was now up to her to live her life fully, tapping the life force flowing through the family tree that Gramma had described.

OTHER CHOICES: SPOKEN AND SILENT DIALOGUES

Whatever feels most natural to you will be the most effective in producing a dialogue. For example, look at a picture of your loved one or simply close your eyes. Some people feel more comfortable talking out loud or silently to themselves rather than writing a dialogue. As with writing, just start talking, as honestly as you can. Don't edit what you are saying, just speak your truth about the relationship. It's important that you pause every once in a while and listen; you may "hear" a response internally.

Marina, an eighty-two-year-old woman, wrote to me after hearing a radio interview in which I spoke about using the imagination to gain access to the living parent within. She wanted to share with me the dramatic breakthrough she had made through talking to her father in her imagination. She would begin her process by closing her eyes and silently talking. It would not be long before she was hearing her father's response. In this way, through a series of dialogues, she began to grieve and heal from the loss of her father; he had moved away when she was a young girl and died years later without permitting her the chance for reconciliation. His absence had profoundly affected her life, for she had been left alone with a mother who was bitter and strict. Over the years after her father's death, Marina became a quiet, passive child, eventually growing into a hesitant and fearful adult.

When Marina began to talk silently with her father, she was shocked to find him so accessible after such a long separation. With each new dialogue, she felt closer to him. After a few weeks, she sensed a dramatic shift within her consciousness. No longer afraid of life, she was confident and inspired to take risks and to connect with other people. Now she initiated a number of creative projects: writing stories was one. In a relatively short time, Marina discovered how much of her life force and creativity had been locked inside her unresolved grief. As her experience dramatically demonstrates, it's never too late to heal a relationship with a deceased loved one and never too late to awaken more fully to life.

At first, Kira Silverbird did not feel ready to converse alone with her father. She felt frightened that he would hit her, as he often had when he was alive. Her first dialogue with her father took place in a therapy session. As her therapist helped move the dialogue along by asking questions and giving support, Kira talked aloud to her father and then gave her father's responses. When Kira told her father, "I hate what you did to me," her therapist interjected, "Can you tell him what he did?"

> KIRA: I hate that you were never there for me. I hate how inaccessible you were. I hate how the only contact I ever had with you was violence and fear. I hate how I had to just go inside myself because I was so scared of you. I'm glad you're dead. I'm glad you can't hit me anymore. I keep thinking I don't have to be scared of you anymore, but I'm still scared.

Kira then spoke her father's words: "I don't want you to be scared of me anymore." As the dialogue proceeded, Kira at times felt overwhelmed by the intensity of her anger and by her father's uncharacteristic responses. At one point, she turned to her therapist. "I feel really lost now. I don't know where to go." He helped her explore what she was feeling toward her father and encouraged her to speak up about everything that was bothering her. By the end of the first dialogue, Kira had stayed with her anger long enough for things to shift with her father. Throughout the dialogue, he had listened diligently to her and responded honestly and respectfully. It was clear to Kira that her father was no longer the man she had known as a child. Wanting to know him better, she stated to her therapist, "I think we're going to be friends." A week later, she felt ready to dialogue with her father alone. She spoke out loud, recording her conversation on tape. Later she transcribed what had transpired.

KIRA: Papa, I'd like to talk to you. Will you come sit with me? Come sit on this side of the bed. Hi. [He's sitting against the wall with his legs stretched out on the bed next to me.] I miss you so much. [Crying] I think of you so much, Papa. It's so weird . . . you're right here, aren't you? Will you talk to me? I want to hear you. I want to be with you. Talk to me.

DAD: I just want to listen now.

KIRA: I have some things to tell you that I could never say before. I feel so sad about how angry I've been all this time, because I'm learning how to get beneath the anger, and I feel so sad that I could never do that with you.

DAD: But you're doing it now.

KIRA: Yeah . . . I want you to hear this so much. I want you to hear how much I love you. [Crying] I was so angry all those years, and all I could tell you was how angry I was. And what I really wanted to say was that I longed to be close to you. When I was a little girl, I wanted you to hold me. I wanted you to sit with me and hold me, and stroke my hair, and tell me about the world, and help me feel safe in the world. I longed to sit in your big lap and feel your big solid hands around me, helping me feel safe. I wanted you to hug me. And it hurt so much when you pushed me away and when you scared me with your anger and your violence. [Crying] That's all I wanted. I didn't want to change you. I didn't want to threaten you or hurt you or compete with you or win any battles. I just wanted to be close.

DAD: Let's be close now.

KIRA: Yeah, I want that with you so much. Dad, just hold me for a while.

DAD: I'm right here.

KIRA: Just hold me. Just be with me. [*To myself:* Let me feel this, and let it in.] I can feel you, Dad. I can almost smell you. I can feel your big hands. Help me heal, Papa. Help me feel what hurts, so that I don't always live stuck in the pain. Just hold my hands and help me feel your presence. Are you really here? Yeah, I feel you. I want you closer. Please come closer. Yeah, that's better. Let me feel you, Papa. [Crying] I miss you so much.

DAD: I haven't gone anywhere.

KIRA: What do you mean, you haven't gone anywhere?

DAD: I can see you right now. You look beautiful.

KIRA: [Crying] Papa, I wanted you to say that to me so many times. I wanted you to tell me that you loved me and that you were proud of me. I wanted you to tell me that you respected me.

DAD: I was too defended.

KIRA: Yeah. I longed for that person underneath all those defenses . . . the person who wrote all those love letters to Mom. I wanted to see that person.

DAD: I couldn't do it.

KIRA: Why couldn't you do it? What was the wall?

DAD: I got hurt too many times.

KIRA: Tell me, Pop, what hurts. Tell me what hurts for you.

DAD: I wanted to be held, too. I wanted to be safe somewhere. It was never safe for me. I didn't know about that. [Crying] I didn't know it was possible to create that for someone.

KIRA: Pop, let me hold *you*. I'll stroke *your* hair. And

you can cry for a little while. I want to give that to you. I want to give it back to you. Mom taught that to me. She taught me how to feel safe. So I can give that to you now. Yeah . . . it's okay to cry. It's okay to let all that pain out. I'm right here with you. Put your arms around me. Thanks. You're with me too . . . I can feel it. I love you, Papa. I love you so much. I just want to rest here with you for a little while. I love you, Papa. I hope I can always feel you like this.

DAD: I'll always be with you when you need me.

KIRA: It's so funny how much I miss you and how much I feel you here at the same time. I'm going to say good-bye now. We'll talk again soon. I love you.

Using internal communication techniques, you can talk out loud or silently to those who have died, thereby connecting with them through your imagination. Some people feel more at ease and unconstrained when they are talking and they would most likely find this choice more conducive to letting their dialogues flow. If you later want to review what has transpired, you can record and transcribe your dialogues.

SPONTANEOUS DIALOGUES

Sometimes the opportunity for an interaction through the imagination arises unexpectedly. A friend of mine was jolted out of sleep by the words, "Good morning, Lois." Shocked, she couldn't believe what she had heard, for Lois knew without a doubt that this was her father's voice. With a sudden outbreak of goose bumps, Lois realized that the morning marked the first anniversary of her father's death. Although she never again heard his voice after this initial startling experience, Lois regularly started talking to her father, afraid that if she hesitated, she would lose this priceless opportunity to connect with him. Lois let her father know how much she missed him and loved him. She updated him on the events of her life since his death and reassured him that her mother was doing well and would soon be joining him. When she finished, she was filled with a deep sense of peace.

A client shared with me another story of an unexpected but meaningful dialogue with a deceased loved one. Janet felt drawn to the site of her husband's grave on the first anniversary of his death. When she arrived at the gravesite and stood silently, reflecting on her loss, a conversation with her husband arose in her imagination—much to her surprise. She spoke out loud to James and heard his responses very clearly in her mind. The two discussed their daughter Claire's upcoming marriage, which James had vehemently opposed when he was alive. Claire's father now wanted to offer his blessing.

Janet was quite shaken by this experience; nothing like this had ever happened to her before. Even though she could not rationally explain the interaction, she was convinced that it had indeed been James she'd spoken with. The next day, she sent Claire a note describing her experience at the cemetery. She enclosed a check to help cover expenses for the wedding that both she and James now fully supported. Claire was deeply moved that she had received the once unattainable approval from her father.

Just as Janet found that standing at her husband's gravesite inspired a dialogue with him, so sitting on her mother's bed instigated Paige to talk with her deceased mother, as though this were the most natural thing in the world. Both her mother and aunt, her last living relatives, had died in a car accident, a loss that felt unbearable to Paige at times. As she describes in her letter to me eleven months after the accident, her talks with her mother gave her so much comfort that she found room for laughter in her grief.

In the first months after Mother's and Aunt Peggy's deaths, I traveled the mile to the house which was home to Mother and

Aunt Peggy. The contents of the home would have to be dissolved . . . but more importantly, their home was my sanctuary.

I sat on the side of my mother's bed and talked to her, cried to her, and asked for her help. Drifting into deep thought, I began to find some peace. I'd busy myself with all the tasks and took comfort from the things that she dearly loved. Reality always returned by 3:00 P.M., as my children needed their mother when they returned from school; they were working through their own grief at the loss of their grandmother and aunt.

Through the process of giving up the home in which I grew up, letting go of the physical bond between mother and daughter, the horror of tragedy, and the sorrow of loss, I never stopped talking to my mother whether it was in my mind when I allowed myself to drift into another world or whether sitting on the corner of the bed with my words spoken aloud.

I felt my mother's presence through the past months, even though I could not touch her or have her put her arms around me to tell me everything would be all right.

I found my mother's wisdom guiding me through the difficult decisions that continued to be made. I also found my mother's essence, a love of laughter and an approach to life in which smiles and laughter can be found in tragedy as well as triumph. I could hear her voice and the tonality of her voice encouraging laughter in spite of my tears. Her index finger waved at me as she told me, "Sell the damn house. . . . I never liked it." We'd laugh together, and we talked in my dreams.

I found that my mother will always be my mother, whether in life or the life after . . . not through memories of our lives together on Earth but by opening the window of my mind to the spiritual world. I hear a phrase, which I am only hearing in part, that my mother used to say to me: "There is more to Heaven and Earth . . ." I guess I should have listened more carefully as a child. She's waving that finger again. Through my tears now, I smile.

Activities that were once shared can suddenly yield an unexpected dialogue. Judy had curled her mother's hair every week for years and did not feel confident that the funeral man could do the job as her mother would have liked. Holding a curling iron, comb, and rollers, she approached her mother's body on the steel table at the funeral home. Her hair was "straight and stiff like an old straw broom"; Judy realized she had a big task ahead of her. She started to comb her mother's hair. "After he [the funeral director] left, I started talking to Mom. After all, we always talked when I did her hair. I didn't see anything wrong with it. I told her her hair was a mess. I told her she would die if she could see it. Then I started to laugh. . . . I worked and talked. Sometimes I worried about the funeral man catching me talking to a dead body. After awhile, though, there was just me and Mom. There were moments when I was sure I heard her voice. The hours passed quickly. It was just like old times" (Ashley, pp. 29–30).

These stories emphasize how important it is to set aside doubts and hesitations when the opportunity for a dialogue presents itself unexpectedly. Lois, Janet, and Paige felt grateful that they had been willing, on a moment's notice, to engage in conversations with their loved ones. These were conversations that shocked but inspired them. Judy felt that it was natural and reassuring to talk to her dead mother as she curled her hair; her only concern was the funeral director's reaction if he should discover what she was doing.

You never know when the opportunity for a dialogue will present itself—upon awakening from sleep, doing a task you once shared, standing at the gravesite. Even though you may be caught off guard or feel self-conscious, seize this precious opportunity for connection.

CREATING A MEMORY BOOK

Ken Kramer, a teacher of religion at San Jose State University, created a book to honor his father, Roy. Bringing a notebook along with him, Ken started writing as his father was dying in the hospital. While his father slept, he wrote poems to his father, reflecting on their relationship, his appreciations, and his regrets. Shortly after Roy's death and the memorial service, Ken gathered together and photocopied these poems along with photos and posters of rifles and engines. On a green paper cover, he placed a smiling photograph of Roy. Above this, Ken typed the words "Old Antique," a term Roy's close friend used to describe his buddy.

Ken feels strongly that creating this book helped him grieve and heal. By the time he completed it and sent copies to friends and family, he felt closer to his father than he had ever felt in life. Ken had actually had a pretty distant relationship with his father; the two had shared few interests and found little to talk about. Much to Ken's delight, death opened up a new, intimate dialogue with his father, as demonstrated by the dialogue between the son and his father that appears toward the end of the book.

s: Dad . . .

f: What, Kenneth? [The exact way he would have said it, I hear, as if he is saying it!]

s: I love you, Dad, even much more now that you are not here. You must feel it. Do you?

f: It is easier, now.

s: Now? Where are you?

f: I don't know, but I think I can know.

s: I can envision you, Dad, still pretty much by yourself even though there are others around you, some of whom you even recognize.

F: [laughs]

S: Dad, I'm collecting material for a Death Book to
    honor you (like the birthday books I have done for
    the girls). Remember the birthday books?

F: Yeah . . .

S: Is there something you would especially want me to
    include in it, something that you are extra proud of?

F: [Pause] Kenneth, ya know that old [pause] ya know!
    It's in the garage. What about that?

Prompted by this dialogue, Ken went to the garage
where he found a small scrapbook tucked inside a larger one.
He had never seen this book before; it was full of news
clippings of incidents of death. As a teacher of a death-and-
dying course at the university, Ken realized that he had inherited his father's fascination with death. He had never
imagined that this interest had been in any way connected
to his father. He then resumed his dialogue.

S: Dad, this is wonderful. Your scrapbook. This is a
    treasure. Now I see where my notebook and journal-
    keeping come from. Now I discover a side of you I
    never, never knew—your preoccupation with death
    news.

After writing this piece, Ken had a significant dream. He
was eating breakfast when his father walked into the room
and sat down on Ken's lap. Roy then got up, walked around
to the other side of the chair, and again sat on his son's lap.
This time he looked deeply into Ken's eyes and kissed him
on the mouth. Ken was deeply moved by his father's uncharacteristic expression of love. The dream confirmed for
Ken that since Roy's death, profound changes had indeed
taken place in his relationship with his father. Weeks after
his father's death, Ken told me that the dialogue initiated
through the book he created continues on in his daily life.

When he sees a photograph of his father, Ken often breaks into spontaneous conversation with him. In the course of our visit over tea, several times Ken spoke lovingly to his father: "You taught me that, Dad!" "Did you hear that, Dad?"

Put together your own memory book using internal communication techniques. Write letters, poems, and dialogues to your loved one. If you sense a response from this person, write that, too. Invite other family members to contribute. You can include photographs, old letters, and quotes from the memorial service or funeral. Dedicate and title your book; create a cover. Then photocopy it. If you want to share your book, send copies to friends and family.

As you use your imagination to create dialogues with a deceased loved one, you will animate and enrich your internal relationship. These dialogues encourage intimate, soul-satisfying conversations—conversations that give voice to your own and another's innermost thoughts and feelings.

CHAPTER 6

Connecting Through Imagery

Writing and talking with a deceased loved one may have already brought you images of this person. In this chapter, I give you some guidance in calling into your imagination and using such images intentionally to connect with the inner presence of the person who has died. With practice, you'll actually be able to see, hear, and touch your loved one. Many clients have told me, "I felt that I was *really* with him. He was so vivid that I could reach out and touch him!"

Imagery, a primal language, is perhaps our first means of perceiving the world. Although we may not be aware of it, we think in imagery all the time. When cultivated, imagery is a powerful tool for healing. I like to think of images as living presences rather than as pictures. When we immerse ourselves in imagery, as we do when we dream, the images surprise, frighten, and fascinate us. They seize our hearts, fix our attention, and even sometimes take our breath away. It is only after we awaken from a dream and look back on it that the dream images become more like pictures. The following suggestions and exercises will help you stake out an image realm in which you can immerse yourself.

Enter your sanctuary space and take some time to settle down and quiet your mind. Then close your eyes and ready yourself by focusing on one image: a flower, a stone, a tree, a fruit. Touch it, smell it, taste it, examine it closely. When you feel satisfied that you have activated your senses through your imagination, move on to the exercises in this chapter. Identify who it is you want to meet. It doesn't matter if this person died recently or many years ago. I will offer three meeting places to help you: in a field, at the heart of a rose, and inside a star. These scenarios will launch you into your meeting in the imagination. Later, you can experiment in creating other sites to work with.

The image of the field, star, or rose acts as a doorway that you must go through. You are entering another world that communicates to you through images. Wait quietly to see what will come, whether in sight, sound, touch, taste, or smell. Imagination will bring you new pictures as well as new sensations of the person who has died. The more details you observe, the more vivid and compelling this experience will be. In fact, you may feel shaken and unnerved by how real this world of the imagination—and the consoling presence of your loved one—seems.

In each of the three exercises, you will first explore the setting, then meet your loved one, and finally let the dialogue and interaction unfold spontaneously. You may find that the person you meet is acting differently than in life. Allow this to happen, paying attention to your own resistance to any new and unfamiliar ways of relating. You may not understand the exchange that occurs while you are performing the exercise, but if you write down the dialogue, you'll have a chance to study it later. Of course, nonverbal communication or silence won't be recordable, so try to keep your memory sharp. Also, the person may want to show you something during your meeting. Be receptive to any images that appear, however absurd, disturbing, or confusing they may be. Trust that your imagination is taking you where you need to go for healing. When you have completed this exercise, spend some time alone in your sanctuary to reflect on what has happened. In particular, notice any changes in your feelings toward the person you have met with in your imagination.

EXERCISE 1

The Field

Close your eyes. Take a few deep breaths and focus on the movement of each breath as it flows in and out of your body. Let the breath be your bridge as you shift your attention from the outer world to an inner world of the imagination.

You are standing in a large field that rolls out to the horizon. You see a figure approaching across this field. As the person comes nearer, you realize this is the one you hoped to meet. Be aware of what you are feeling. Notice how this person looks and moves, what he or she is wearing. Has the person changed? Be willing to let go of old pictures; your loved one may look and act in a different way than you remember. Stay in the present with this person, letting your interaction unfold without editing or interfering with what happens. Let your loved one know how you have felt since the death: what you miss, what you regret, what you appreciate about him or her. Update the person on what has changed for you since the death, and take time to listen to all responses and messages. Follow this exchange wherever it may go.

When you feel ready, tell your loved one good-bye. Watch as the person leaves, remaining aware of how you are feeling. Spend some time alone with yourself, reflecting on this experience. Then, open your eyes.

EXERCISE 2

The Rose

Closing your eyes, imagine a rosebud that is still tightly closed. Use all your inner senses to experience this flower: What color is it? How does it feel?

The rose is now beginning to open slowly, petal by petal. At its center stands your loved one, waiting for you. Go to meet the person and allow your interaction to unfold on its own. You may be surprised at what happens between you. Some interaction or communication could take place that you never imagined possible in life.

This is a time to update your relationship. Share with this person the changes, feelings, insights, and new perspectives you have experienced since the death.

When you are ready, conclude your visit. If you still feel unfinished, let the person know when you will be visiting again. Then step out of the rose's center and watch the petals fold up again, enclosing and protecting the place of your meeting.

EXERCISE 3

The Star

Close your eyes and imagine yourself sitting on a hill. Above you stretches the night sky with thousands of stars glimmering against a background of black. Thinking of a loved one who has died, let your eyes wander over the entire sky until one star begins to stand out. Looking at this star, observe the threads of light that emanate from its center. One of these threads shines down to where you sit. Follow this beam up to the star. As you move closer and closer, the intense light may blind or overwhelm you. It may take some time for your eyes to adjust.

When you reach the star, step into its center. Your loved one will be waiting for you. Take all the time you need to get reacquainted. Discuss any unfinished business between you; share resentments and regrets as well as appreciations. Then explore your relationship as it is now. Acknowledge the changes, no matter how subtle.

As you prepare to leave, you will be presented with a gift to take back with you. Receive this and descend back to Earth on the thread of light.

SUE'S STORY

Imagery has the power to connect the living and the dead within the imagination. This connection takes place on many levels at once, making it a profoundly moving and transforming experience. You not only hear the words of the person you had thought lost to you, but you can also see and touch this person. In holding the image of this person in your mind, you create and re-create the relationship, not necessarily as it was but as it is now.

I saw my father two years after his death. I found myself in an old rose garden with climbing vines, old gnarled trees, and tangled roses. At first, I embraced an oak tree until an old rose-bush called to me. He was the grandfather rose of the garden, planted in dark, rich soil; his trunk was twisted and knotted, his leaves covered in lemon-white flowers tinged with crimson. I bent toward the fragrance and saw one rose open. My father stepped from its center and grew to his full height.

My father wore a beige, yellow, and gray Pendleton shirt and tan khakis; he slowly took off his glasses, put them in his pocket, and took my hand. I noticed his long, tapered fingers, still artistic and yet covered with wrinkles and tanned from working in the garden. I told him how much I loved him, and we hugged each other easily, unlike years ago when it was so awkward. Then I asked my father to hold me in a rocking chair. He said he would love to, that he tried to hold me when I was a child, but I was too active and eager to jump off his lap to play outdoors.

A wooden rocking chair appeared with gold stenciling on the back like the one in our den at home. Down we sat. I could feel the soft yet rough texture of the Pendleton against my cheek, its pocket and buttons. My father smelled clean like Camay soap.

Then we walked together, holding hands. I told him of my complete love, joy, and peace in his presence. We turned to each other and, as we did, the past and all its pain vanished. "Daddy, my God! We have healed the past. We have healed the past for us both. All that matters is the love I feel for you and the love you feel for me." My father asked for my forgiveness for the suffering he had caused me; he cried and hung his head. I raised his dear face in my hands and said: "All is forgiven. I know you did the very best you could and now is all that matters."

We sat on an old tree stump in the garden, relishing each other's company, laughing and talking. Soon it was time to go and I helped him step into the rose, and it enclosed him once more. I kissed and blessed the rose, thanked it for holding my father in its embrace. "Good-bye, Daddy. I'll be back." I walked out of the garden into the trees, feeling the wind swirling around me.

CANDACE'S STORY

Candace's father died the first time for her when she was three years old. He joined the U.S. Navy and left to fight in the war. Her gentle father returned an incurable and irresponsible alcoholic. By the time he died twenty years later, Candace had already given her father up for dead. At the time of her father's death, Candace was pregnant, and her obstetrician advised her not to go to the funeral, for fear that the stress would be too much. She was secretly relieved at his counsel, but years later, her unresolved grief surfaced and made itself known through a debilitating physical ailment. In finally facing the loss of her father, she turned to meditation, prayer, dreams, painting, and writing activities, which often yielded rich imagery. A clear mind, empty page, and blank canvas are all fertile arenas where healing images can take form. In a class, she was introduced to the rose exercise.

The rose in my garden is withered and dead-looking, faded cream without much hue, most petals already fallen to the ground. It seems appropriate. Nevertheless, I ask for it to open, and as I do, before my eyes the rose metamorphoses into a large and splendidly beautiful, healthy flower. Out steps my father, a young man in his late twenties. We sit down on my patio. I begin to vent my anger at him for abandoning me and ruining my life. I expected nothing from him this time, either, but I waited to see what might happen.

I find myself on the front steps of St. Patrick's Cathedral in New York. I walk to the doors, open them, and see my father, a bishop in full regalia, walking down the aisle toward me but oblivious of my presence. Back on the patio, I say to him, "I had no idea you wanted to be a priest!" He tells me that his unfulfilled dream of becoming a medical doctor was not so far afield. Medicine was the more acceptable path to pursue; he followed neither.

Next I am on the shore of a large, rustic lake in St. Louis. A boy, all in white and wearing knickers and a tie, is standing in a small wooden boat. He is helping a girl, dressed in soft, filmy, white cotton, climb into the boat. I am straining to see if it is my mother. Again, much to my amazement, she is a lovely child with whom he is much in love, not my mother. I hear him say about my mother, "She was insufferably vain!" I recognize his frustration and empathize with his recognition. My mother had told me reams of stories of how she was wooed by this and that man and how she settled for my father. Never once did I hear about my father's past.

"But who is this girl?" I ask him. He tells me he knew her for years. She eventually married a wealthy man who would take care of her. After my dad married my mother, he saw this friend once or twice, but he stayed married to my mother, largely because of me, he said, and because divorce was absolutely unacceptable in his eyes and to his family and the Catholic church.

I find myself in a bright and airy bedroom of a large Victorian home. I see the high ceilings, an open window facing the tree-lined street as a curtain blows gently in the breeze. I see no one, but I sense my dad is there alone. The room feels lonely. Has someone died? Yes, my grandfather has died, and his son is in the vacated death room, desperately trying to sort out a loss that is too large for this twelve-year-old boy and youngest of six to hold. I get the sense that the boy was not allowed in the room earlier to say good-bye to the dying man.

Next it is World War II, and my dad is a battleship navigator in the South Pacific. The day is spring clear, warm and sunny. Suddenly I get this picture of a very tan and healthy-looking man who says to me: "I actually liked being in the Navy. I had to admit to myself at this time that, although I missed you and your mother terribly, I also liked being away from your mother and grandmother." My mother's mother had been loving but controlling; she never was to relinquish her daughter to a man. I begin to cry tears of compassion and understanding. I had only heard my mother's side of the stories.

I am invisible in the St. Louis kitchen; my dad in uniform, mother and grandmother are seated at the table. Daddy is saying he wants to leave. He cannot imagine how the marriage can ever work. He doesn't want to hurt anyone. My mother and grandmother are manipulating the situation; my father succumbs and agrees to stay. He returns from his leave back to the war. This comes as sheer news to me that he had ever tried to end an even-then unworkable relationship. My parents had seemed so happy to me as a little girl.

The last thing I do in this meeting is to tell Daddy how sorry I am for the way his life turned out. I am feeling more forgiving and less accusatory. Then my father says to me, "I am so sorry!" I know he is, but for so many years I have refused that. Being sorry doesn't change anything; what it can do is get someone pretty easily off the hook. So I tell him I want to be released. I want him to do whatever he can wherever he is, over there or in a new life, to make it up to me. Release me and in so doing, release himself.

As for so many people, in this encounter, the images did not unfold as Candace had expected. They seemed to have a life of their own as they led her through vignettes of her father's life. Having worked with active imagination techniques before, Candace trusted the flow of imagery and was careful not to interfere. By the end of the exercise, she felt that for the first time, she had experienced her father's life through his eyes rather than through her mother's.

These images were both unnerving and healing for Candace. They allowed her to contact her father in a caring and compassionate way; the person she spoke to was the kind, caring, sensitive, wise, and highly intelligent man she had known as a young girl. Through the vivid vignettes, she was able to experience her father's disappointments and unlived dreams and for the first time to understand the factors that had contributed to his alcoholism.

Through the imagination, you can enter another's body or life experiences, making it possible to experience the world through that person's eyes. In this way, empathy develops naturally, transforming old hurts and resentments into understanding and compassion.

MEETING A SON/MEETING A MOTHER

Richard started therapy when stress at work began to endanger his health. After a few sessions, it became clear that underlying his stress was the somber presence of a grief he felt hopeless to resolve: his son, Brian, had died of AIDS five years before. It had been devastating for Richard to watch Brian's body deteriorate and to helplessly witness his suffering. These memories haunted him by day, and grief gnawed mercilessly at his gut at night.

In one of our sessions, though doubtful, Richard agreed to try the rose exercise. To his great surprise, a clear image of Brian manifested itself as soon as the rose opened. Brian smiled and assured Richard that he was at peace; he reported that he had felt frustrated trying to let his father know this. They proceeded to talk about their relationship, healing some old wounds that had plagued them both for years. When Richard opened his eyes, he looked immensely relieved: his face was clear and radiant, qualities that often accompany a dramatic opening of the heart. Richard told me he only regretted having waited so long to come to this place of healing. He had never dreamed this kind of breakthrough was possible by means of the imagination.

Another client, Lela, chose the field exercise, hoping to meet Anya, her mother, who had died several months earlier. Lela had not been present when Anya passed away. She had left the hospital for a dinner break, returning to find her mother gone. Ever since, she had agonized over being absent at the time of Anya's passing and had obsessed over what she could have done to keep her mother alive. Originally, Anya's decline resulted from a simple accident from which Lela had expected her mother to recover easily. However, as unforeseen complications set in, Anya's health and spirits rapidly deteriorated. Lela regretted that she had not been aggressive enough with the doctors, that she had not pushed for other medical options. Over and over in her head, Lela would replay the progression of her mother's illness, condemning herself for all the mistakes she felt she had made.

Now, as she focused on the field in her imagination, Lela saw her mother as clearly as though she were alive. As soon as Anya appeared, the images became brilliant. Lela talked with her mother for a long time about her guilt and anguish, and then listened to what Anya had to say. Anya told her that she had wanted to die. Having concluded her commitments and knowing that her children were taken care of, she had felt ready for this step into the unknown. She had avoided telling Lela about this decision because she knew her daughter would resist.

Anya's words astounded Lela, yet she knew her mother's perception was true. If, in real life, Anya had told her that she wanted to die, Lela would have resisted and fought, completely unready to let her mother go. Anya's revelation released Lela from her guilt, and in its place, she experienced a deep love for her mother. Lela was finally able to focus on letting Anya go.

Healing consists in receiving—rather than repressing—the images that the imagination sets before us. Setting aside their assumptions and expectations, Richard and Lela embraced their loved ones—and their messages—as they appeared in the exercises. These potent images brought Richard and Lela to the edge of the known and restored the family members lost to them.

A MOTHER MEETS HER BABY

Randi's baby was stillborn, taken away from her while Randi was still drowsy from medication. She never had an opportunity to see her child, to hold him, or say good-bye. Upon returning home, Randi collapsed into a deep, debilitating grief. In her dreams, she desperately searched for her baby in the hospital but never found him. In waking hours, she felt depressed, ate little, and cried constantly. Her husband, concerned when months had passed and she was still unwilling to leave the house, encouraged Randi to seek counseling. In our sessions, we explored the terrain of her grief. Since words were difficult for her and imagination was richly activated in her grief, Randi found imagery exercises to be very beneficial to her healing. For those of you who do not like to write or speak, imagery is a valuable route to explore internal communication.

In one session, I had Randi close her eyes while I guided her into the night sky. One bright star caught her attention, and she climbed a luminous ladder of light toward it. As soon as she stepped into the star's center, Jesus appeared before her, enveloped in a bright golden light. Wrapped in a white blanket, her baby lay cradled in his arms. She let out a cry and reached for her child. In her imagination, with her baby in her arms, the dead child became real. Randi stroked the tiny fingers and kissed the downy head. For a long time, Randi held her child and talked to him. When it was time for her to leave, Jesus silently stepped forward and held out his hands. This time she gave up her baby with a profound sense of peace and trust. Now, when she looks up at the night sky, Randi thinks of her baby and knows that he is shining there as a brilliant star. Her experience reminds me of the parting words of the little prince to his friend: "In one of the stars I shall be living. In one of them I shall be laughing. . . . And when your sorrow is comforted (time soothes all sorrows) you will be content that you have known me. You will always be my friend" (Antoine de Saint-Exupery, p. 85).

THE POWER OF IMAGERY: A REVIEW

As we prepare a fertile environment for imagery to come forth, the wise imagination yields to us the very images that we need for healing. Trust these images; receive and embrace them; experience them with all your senses. The more detail you focus on, the more powerful, immediate, and compelling this experience will be. Open yourself to the shock of wonder and joy. Whenever your intellect interferes by judging or editing, gently bring your awareness back to the flow of images. Treasure and savor the images that come to you; revel in their healing touch. Let them work on you long after the exercise is over. If you carry inside images of your loved one, they may imbue your day with the presence of the other. You may also want to treat these episodes as you would movie clips, which encompass meanings to think about later.

Let's review the steps for working with internal communication through imagery:

- Identify who you wish to see, and think about the problems and unresolved issues in your relationship. How have these affected your feelings about this person since the death?
- Set aside a period of uninterrupted time in your sanctuary. Sit down, focusing your attention on your breathing. Let your mind clear and your body settle.
- Close your eyes and, in your imagination, go to a healing place (such as a garden, field, forest, special room, or beach). Explore this environment with all your senses.
- Invite the person to visit you in the place you have cho-

sen for the purpose of healing your relationship. Watch carefully as he or she approaches. Be aware of how you are feeling.

- Begin a dialogue, addressing the issues of concern to you. Speak honestly. Don't interfere with what naturally unfolds. You can also just be with this person, sharing the time together in silence.
- Listen carefully and respectfully to the response.
- Be receptive to unexpected developments. For example, the person may take you somewhere or give you something. Someone else may appear.
- Bring your encounter to a close. If you still feel unfinished, tell your family member that you will soon be meeting again in your imagination.
- Spend some time in your sanctuary after the person has departed. Relax and reflect on what has happened.
- Write down what you have experienced. It may take time to understand the meaning or significance of what happened.

PART 3

Reaching Outward

The only thing keeping you from deep, satisfying, soulful relationships is your imagination.
THOMAS MOORE

Chapter 7

Family Communication After a Death

Liana sank with a sigh into the brown armchair in my office. It seemed that she had used up what little reserve of energy she had to get to this appointment. Her first words confirmed this: "I've been waiting all week for this appointment. I can't tell you what it means to me right now to feel that I'm in a safe place." She paused, taking a big breath. For a fleeting moment, it was as if the brown eyes that had been taking me in suddenly opened into tunnels, and I could see the pain held in her heart. Instinctively, she looked into her lap where her hands were clasped. As with so many of my clients and friends, Liana had learned to retreat when waves of feeling welled up. She felt ashamed of her rawness and vulnerability. "I'm glad you're here," I told her softly and she looked up again, reassured.

Then her story spilled out of her, like water from a reservoir that has accumulated over many storms.

I feel so alone. There's an ache in my chest that won't go away, even when I'm with my husband and children. It's scary to feel this alone. My father died nine months ago. His death was a huge loss, much bigger than I had thought it would be. We had been very close. It wasn't until he died that I realized how much I had taken for granted his quiet support. I miss him terribly.

Now what's concerning me most is my relationship with my mother. I realized soon after my dad died that I wanted to heal this relationship, with all its years of pain and anger, because she is the only parent I have left. I remember thinking, "Oh my God, if my mom dies now, it'll be so much worse. It'll be by far the worst loss I have ever gone through because I will not have reconciled. We will never have an understanding of each other."

After my father's death, there have been huge explosions between my mother and me. Suddenly, I saw the dynamics of our relationship so clearly. We've danced around each other for years, without really seeing one another. And when my father died, I felt I was finally seeing my mother—and I didn't like what I saw. I didn't respect or like her. I felt she was narcissistic and too insecure to stand on her own. The thought of being like her really scared me. I realized I had lost the one parent who could support me emotionally. I was angry at being left with a parent who I thought didn't understand me. A few months ago, I tried to tell her what I was going through in my grief, but she couldn't hear me. She was too caught up in her own grief. At that time, I said some hurtful things. I just don't have the energy to be considerate and careful around her, as I always have been. I see now how I've played a game of being the good daughter at the expense of being myself with her.

It's agonizing now to get together with her. I can no longer play the old roles, and so we don't know how to be with one another. We're both at a loss, and we just feel lonely when we're together. I want so much to feel love for her. I want to be able to forgive her for . . ."

Liana's voice trailed off, and her eyes, which had been fixed on me throughout her story, now gazed back down at her hands. She had caught herself just as she was about to blurt out some family secrets. This was territory she was unready to venture into as yet, and I respected that. We'd come back to this in a later session. When she looked up, I nodded. She looked relieved as she continued her story.

My brother has cut off all communication with my mother and me because he is going through a terrible time. He's working through his grief and the fact that he didn't reconcile with my father. It's hard to believe, but he took things a lot harder than I did. I know my mother is having a hard time understanding this. I'm sometimes caught in the middle, but I think I understand what he's doing, so I can respect his need to become comfortable with saying, "Sorry, but I can't deal with this right now." He's entitled to that, and it's no reason for him to feel guilty. It's not my job to take care of him. You can't shelter people from their pain. But I miss him so much. It's tragic that our family is so cut off from one another at the time we all need one another so much.

I had hoped my husband would help me out of my pain and loneliness, but we've had trouble communicating, too. He tries to be supportive, but he's never lost a parent, and he has no idea about what I'm going through. He seems intimidated by the intensity of my emotions. And I'm realizing now that I don't really trust him with my feelings, especially when they are so raw and vulnerable. Too many times he's been sarcastic with me. I feel so alone.

Bringing her hand to her chest, Liana held it over the place where her heart was hurting. She broke into loud sobs. Her anguish was so excruciating that I could understand why her husband had withdrawn from her. I took a big breath. I couldn't take her pain away, nor did I want to. It was important that she experience it fully in that moment in the presence of another human being who also knew that pain. I encouraged her to let the tears come; I knew that her tears were leading her back to herself.

How Grief Changes Families

Grief affects different kinds of family systems in different ways, so I'll limit my remarks here to the family of origin, focusing on marriages and other partnerships in chapter 8.

In an earlier chapter, I suggested that with grief comes a heightened capacity to recognize conditioning and patterns of relationship with great clarity. Painful insights into issues that may have been overlooked or avoided now slip past lowered defense mechanisms and problems become magnified. I have been impressed with the number of my clients and interviewees who have used the following metaphor: "Since the death, it's as though a veil has been lifted. I'm seeing everything differently." This clear sight is an opportunity to appreciate the strengths of a relationship, to address its unhealthy aspects, and to develop more authentic ways of relating. The sense of freedom and new possibilities in the relationship can be exciting and terrifying.

This shift in perspective plus a sense of her own aloneness contributed to the changes Liana was experiencing in her relationships within her family. In her loneliness, she had been thrown back on herself and had been forced to evaluate relationships she had previously taken for granted. It was painful for her to see the compromises she had made in her relationship with her mother and husband and to face the absence of support and intimacy in both, especially at such a significant time of loss. As with many people who are grieving, Liana felt a yearning to improve and deepen her relationships. In particular, she knew that she wanted a more loving and authentic relationship with her mother, but with so much anger and resentment constantly surfacing, Liana had no idea how to begin.

As Liana's story demonstrated, a system in place over many years can be thrown into chaos and upheaval after the

death of a family member. Old patterns don't work with the
same results; past resentments, rivalries, and jealousies surface. Along with unresolved issues that may go back to childhood, new tensions and resentments can build up over issues
of care for the dying person. Also—famously—the distri-
bution of the estate of the deceased may become a major
area of contention, fostering anger and family feuds.

Furthermore, alliances within the family shift after the
death, creating new dynamics in the family pattern. For example, a client, Derrick, described the profound changes he
had experienced in his relationship with his brother since his
father's death. Derrick's brother and father had been very
close, and Derrick had felt overpowered and overshadowed
by his brother. However, when their father died, the family
constellation changed. Suddenly, the brother was left without
an ally and therefore with less power than before. Derrick
felt confident in standing up to his brother and fully expressing his own talents.

As families undergo such shifts, fighting may increase.
Many feel confused by and even ashamed of this fighting. If
family members can focus on the underlying issues and communicate with one another, this can be a time to create
healthier relationships.

Finally, the awareness of mortality that death brings can
be a powerful incentive to work on family relationships. Liana's realization that she had only one parent left motivated
her to work on healing her relationship with her mother,
despite the pain and anger her efforts brought her. The
death of one parent often breaks through our resistances and
hesitancies in making necessary changes with the other. Nate
told me how the death of his father had forced him to look
at and change ways that he had related to his mother. The
close relationship with his father had allowed him to overlook
the difficulties with his mother. "My greatest fear in losing
my mother is that I will spend a lot of time feeling very
repentant about not treating her better. If she were to die

today, I would wish that I had been more patient, less judgmental. Every day I think about this and I think there's a way to prevent that kind of regret and remorse. I work toward it; I've made improvements in a few months."

Changes occur with siblings, too. The death of a family member can bring siblings together with a new appreciation for this special family bond, and increased willingness and incentive may surface to work through unresolved issues toward more clarity and connection. Siblings may feel freer to talk about childhood rivalries, jealousies, and secrets that may have contaminated the current relationship. With so much coming to the surface, this is a powerful time to heal these grudges and establish a mature adult relationship with one another. In *In Memoriam*, Henri Nouwen writes about the transforming effect his mother's death had on his relationship with his siblings: "This new closeness that we began to feel was something far greater than what is expressed by the remark, 'You still have each other.' We became for each other new people with new lives and new perspectives. Life started to reveal itself in new ways. I was not simply saying farewell to her; I was also letting go of something in myself that had to die. I also perceived this in my father, my brothers and my sister. Old boundaries that had maintained certain distances between us were being lifted so that new intimacies could grow" (Nouwen, p. 37).

Sometimes there is the opportunity to get to know a family member with whom the relationship had been more distant. A woman in one of my workshops had never spent any time alone with her father. She did not know who he was as an individual, apart from his role in his marriage. Whenever her father had answered her telephone calls home, he had automatically handed the phone to her mother.

After her mother's death, my client felt awkward at first whenever she was alone with her father. As the weeks passed, though, she felt excited about getting to know him and started to enjoy spending time with him. When he died six months later of a heart attack, she felt grateful for this brief quality time together.

Still, there can be difficulties: fights, regrets, and resentments with a remaining parent or sibling. With both grieving simultaneously but in different ways, interactions can take on an intensity and rawness that had not been present before. With the new clarity of vision resulting from the crises, the adult child may be unable to ignore unhealthy patterns or issues in the relationship that had been long suppressed. Discussions, confrontations, and—it is to be hoped—breakthroughs can be the fascinating and productive result.

HOW TO MAKE CHANGES

How can we effect the changes we desire in the midst of the emotional chaos that grief brings to a family? Communicating with family members and friends can be very hard during grief. Emotions are stirred up then, and people often feel raw and on edge. Those who are grieving often act in ways that would seem unthinkable at other times, expressing anger, impatience, and other negative emotions. They take risks and speak their minds with sometimes brutal honesty. They do not have the energy for being nice, taking care of other people's feelings, holding back, or engaging in old, unproductive behavior patterns. There can be a sense of liberation for those who are grieving as they discover that they actually feel better when they express themselves truthfully and authentically. If family members are all grieving at the same time, it is common for fights to break out, misunderstandings to take place, and even contact to be severed. Those outside the circle may be shocked and disturbed by these changes in behavior, and this can have a destructive effect on communication as well.

WITHDRAWAL

Where fighting surfaces, temporary withdrawal from the relationship can be a powerful tool. Still, it can be hard to trust that pulling back from a living parent or sibling may eventually generate healing and the desire to reconnect. I experienced this uncertainty personally after my father died. The power of the forces of grief erupting in me then would not let me set aside my own feelings to focus on my mother's needs. I needed to pull back from my mother in order to honor and fully experience my own grief. Since childhood, I had been conditioned to take care of my mother's needs before my own, and this pattern had become so woven into the fabric of our relationship that I did not even see the full extent of it until after my father's death—humbling for a therapist to admit. While this awareness and the ensuing change in my behavior created great discomfort at the time, I felt grateful for the developmental push my grief delivered to me. Not only did my mother and I connect again months later with a new appreciation for our differences, but I experienced an appreciable shift in making my needs count in my other relationships as well.

While distancing can provide a breathing space, it is important that it be a phase in creation of change, not a permanent stance. Author and psychotherapist Harriet Lerner advises in *The Dance of Intimacy*, "Slowly moving toward more connectedness rather than more distance with members of our own kinship group is one of the best insurance policies for bringing a more solid sense of self to other relationships. When we have few connections with extended family, and one or more cutoffs with a nuclear family member (a sibling or parent), our other relationships may resemble a pressure cooker, particularly if we start a family of our own. The degree to which we are distant and cut off from our first family is directly related to the amount of intensity and reactivity we bring to other relationships." (Lerner, p. 214).

USING INTERNAL COMMUNICATION

Although external communication at such an emotionally charged time may contribute to increased tension and fighting, the same resources that enable reconnection with the deceased can help us link to our living family members in a new and strengthened way. Imagination provides a safe place to pull back, reassess, and experience the relationship inwardly, and internal communication affords the opportunity to do the healing work.

Where communication has broken down or has been cut off by grief, imagination can build a bridge between you and a family member across a chasm of hurt, disappointment, misunderstanding, and anger. As you have seen, in your imagination, you have freedom to address issues that have been silenced, to express yourself without restriction, and to give voice to repressed feelings. You can step inside another and experience the relationship through his or her eyes, since in the imagination you are not limited to one body. And you can watch *yourself* in the relationship while simultaneously participating in it.

All this you can do within yourself, without the other's participation: a remarkable opportunity when communication seems impossible in everyday life. In offering fresh resources to break through destructive patterns of relating and new perspectives that foster compassion and understanding, the imagination will help you deepen bonds, heal rifts, and express love in ways that you never dreamed possible in your everyday experience.

Sometimes, work with the imagination within a family results in surprising changes in the other person. A client used ex-

ercise 1, presented later in this chapter, to talk to her living
father about issues in their relationship that had driven them
apart for years. Their communication had become limited to a
few superficial gruff exchanges. A few days after doing this exercise, she talked to him on the phone and then reported to me,
"I couldn't *believe* how he listened to me. He's never done that
before. We talked about several important issues without
screaming at each other. Something has opened up in our communication that I didn't think was possible."

Practice in the imagination not only lays the groundwork
for an external discussion with a living family member but
also seems to affect the discussion itself. After a confronta-
tion with her sister, one of my clients told me, "After my
mother died, I could no longer ignore the conflicts between
my sister and me. Since she was the only member of my
family left, I wanted a closer relationship with her. For
weeks, I confronted my sister in my imagination, using internal communication techniques my therapist had taught
me. As I gained more clarity about my needs as well as compassion for her failings, I felt ready to talk to her. My discussion with my sister turned out very much like one I had
had in my imagination. My sister was willing to listen to me.
Usually, she cuts me right off if I'm telling her anything that
might be in any way critical of my father. But this time, she
was more receptive and understanding than any other time
I can remember. Our relationship is different now. For the
first time in my life, I feel at ease with my sister."

In tapping the imagination, we access a much greater
knowledge than our conscious mind can grasp. Therefore, it
is critical that you approach this work with humility and receptivity. As with your work with a deceased loved one, set
aside any preconceived ideas of content or outcome, and
avoid imposing what you want. Dare to receive whatever
happens without judging or editing it. Allow yourself to be
stretched. Images may occur that surprise, fascinate, and
even horrify you. The imagination is naturally open and cre-

ative. It doesn't differentiate between negative and positive, between ecstatic and horrific, between life and death. It encompasses all this, moving us past the borders of our limited perspectives and offering the potential for healing beyond our wildest dreams.

Throughout this and succeeding chapters, guided exercises using internal communication will help you voice unexpressed feelings, gain new understanding and compassion, and face and reexperience negative situations that are currently affecting a relationship with a living family member. As you practice internal communication, you'll find yourself getting better at it, speaking out and listening more easily within your imagination. But the benefits will not stop there. Confronting a loved one in your imagination will give you the confidence to take more risks externally: to speak honestly, set boundaries, and ask for what you want. For this reason, after working with the internal communication techniques described here, you may want to initiate a face-to-face conversation with the family member in order to integrate new breakthroughs, understandings, and insights into your relationship. Keep the list of questions below nearby in order to assess your readiness to talk to the person. Then, define your goals, identify your topics, make the initial contact, pick a safe place, and set guidelines for a productive and healing discussion.

RECLAIMING FREEDOMS

Writer and public speaker John Bradshaw describes five freedoms based on the work of family therapist Virginia Satir that he claims are essential to healthy relationships in a family: the freedom to

- See and hear
- Say what one thinks and feels

- Feel what one feels
- Ask for what one wants
- Take risks for oneself

In creating healthy family relationships, a person needs to reclaim these specific freedoms.

The following exercise will help you regain these freedoms—or claim them within your living relationship for the first time—through internal communication. Start by setting aside an uninterrupted period of time in your sanctuary. Review the questions below, which are designed to focus your attention on the work at hand. Then, perhaps using a picture of the family member you will be focusing on in this exercise, follow the procedure closely.

ASSESSING FAMILY RELATIONSHIPS

- What qualities are now important to me in my relationship?
- What am I unwilling to put up with anymore?
- Am I satisfied with the quality of my relationships?
- What changes have occurred in my relationship with family members? What do I want in my relationships with them?
- As roles and responsibilities change as a result of the death, have any resentments or appreciations remained unexpressed?
- Has the living relationship been affected by the death?
- In going through this period of stress and grief, what strengths and weaknesses have merged in the living relationship?
- What patterns in my parents' marriage do I see reflected in this relationship with a living family member?

- How have my friendships changed? Which friendships have grown closer? Grown apart?
- Am I willing to let my family and friends know what I want in my relationships? Am I able to express to them what I think and feel?
- Am I successful in becoming closer to my family and friends? In setting boundaries with them?
- How authentic am I able to be? How much have I compromised myself? Am I able to take risks in my relationships to attain what I want?

Once you reflect on these questions and clarify your priorities, you can take steps to align your relationships with your deepest longings. But there's a cautionary note: as you begin to act, be prepared for considerable disruption and conflict in your relationships.

EXERCISE 1

An Internal Encounter

To perform the exercise, sit down, close your eyes, and bring your awareness to your breathing for a few minutes to settle your body and mind. Now, imagine a healing place. This can be a place you have seen or visited in ordinary reality, or it may be a place that exists solely in your imagination. Perhaps it exists in nature—a forest, beach, waterfall, mountaintop, garden—or it might be a special room. You may decide on one particular place only to find that another image presents itself instead. Don't fight this; trust what happens spontaneously.

Experience this place with all your senses. Look around you and pay attention to details. Touch, smell, listen. Activating your inner senses is a critical step in this exercise. The more fully attuned you are in your imagination to all your senses, the more intense this experience will be. Continue to explore this environment with your senses until you feel fully present in this place.

When you feel ready, invite the chosen person from your family to join you in this healing environment. As this individual approaches, focus your awareness on any physical sensations you are experiencing. Rather than anticipating what may happen, pay close attention to the person's expression, movements, and dress. Be aware of what you are feeling.

Some people, feeling too anxious to talk with the family member alone, even in the imagination, ask for a guide to support and protect them. Standing beside you or behind you, this guide may not actively participate in this encounter, but may help you simply by being present.

Begin to address the issues that are of concern to you in your relationship with your family member. Speak honestly and authentically, expressing your feelings fully. This is your opportunity to speak up about the neglected or taboo areas of your relationship.

If you are bringing up an event from the past that you want to resolve, you may want to talk about what happened, how you felt—and feel—about it, how this event affected you, and what you want the person to do about it now. For the best results, avoid blaming, manipulating, or demanding. Still, feel free to express your anger, maintaining your awareness of the sensations in your body. Do this as directly and cleanly as you can. This expression of feeling is for your own healing, not to create a reaction in the other person.

Next, allow your family member to respond. Listen carefully and respectfully. Let the dialogue and interaction unfold spontaneously; don't interfere. You may find that your family member is acting differently from ever before. Let this happen. Notice your own resistance to new and unfamiliar ways of relating. You may not understand what is being said. There may be nonverbal communication; there may be silence. Other things may begin to happen. The person—or your guide—may want to show you something. Be receptive to any images that appear. They may seem absurd, disturbing, or confusing, but trust that the imagination is taking you where you need to go for healing. In tapping the imagination, we gain access to a much greater knowledge than our conscious mind can grasp.

For a deeper understanding of your family member's perceptions of and feelings about your relationship, you can step inside that person's body. Look out at the world through his or her eyes. How have you been wounded? How have you struggled in this relationship? What do you want from the person (you, in your own body) standing in front of you? What do you want to say to this person? Allow a dialogue to develop between the you within the other person and the you relating to that person.

You may find that your meeting begins to move beyond the personal into more soulful concerns. This is not surprising, for the imagination is soul territory and, as Thomas Moore points out, relationships, particularly intensely entangled ones, can lead to the revelation of soul. He writes, "Even though we may think our strong emotions focus on the people around us, we are being set face to face with divinity itself, however we understand or speak about that mystery" (Moore, p. 257).

As your encounter with your family member comes to a close, say good-bye. If you still feel incomplete, let the person know that you will be meeting

again in the imagination. Watch your family member
leave, being fully aware of all that is going on inside
of you. Then, spend some time alone in your imaginary healing place, reflecting on what has happened
and on how you feel now. How have your feelings
changed toward this person? Relax and absorb the
healing in this place: in your imagination, lie down in
the grass, bathe in a waterfall or spring, swim in the
ocean, climb into a warm bed, feast on a meal.

When you open your eyes, record your experience in
your journal to help you integrate it. In the following days
and weeks, notice any changes that manifest in your relationship. As you clear away the inner barriers to change and
transformation, you may find that you feel differently about
and relate differently to this person. Explore ways you can
act to support these changes. You may choose to talk with
the person directly about some of the issues you explored in
your imagination. Again, don't make assumptions about how
he or she will react to you. Be open and receptive.

When Liana first tried this exercise in a therapy session,
she was amazed by the intensity of anger she felt and expressed toward her mother. She spoke of hurts and disappointments she had never spoken of before. She was
experiencing those very freedoms that Satir identifies as essential to healthy family relationships: the freedom to say
what she thought and felt and to take risks for herself. In
the exercise, her mother simply listened; she didn't interrupt,
break down in tears, or give excuses. She nodded and listened intently, as though she understood. Feeling her
mother had heard her, Liana felt so much love and tenderness after their internal encounter that she reached out to
her mother and hugged her. As she held her mother, she
could feel her mother's heart beating close to her own.

The next time Liana performed this exercise, her mother spoke to her, sharing the concerns and difficulties that she had experienced as a mother and wife. It was a breakthrough for Liana to step inside her mother and experience the relationship through her eyes. She realized then how much her mother loved and cared for her. She understood how her mother's childhood wounds had crippled her emotionally, making it difficult for her to express love without narcissism or criticism.

EXERCISE 2

An External Encounter

Once you have worked with internal communication to the point that you feel clear and compassionate, you can move on to external communication. First, assess your readiness by answering the following questions:

- Am I clear about what I want in this relationship?
- Do I still feel very upset about the issues I addressed using internal communication?
- Am I able to speak out truthfully and listen respectfully?
- Am I able to open to the other person's point of view?

Take some time to reflect on the areas of difficulty you have with your family member. Ask yourself: "What past or present issues are inhibiting a clear, close, and respectful relationship? Where do I stand on these issues? What do I want? What do I want to change? What part have I played?"

Then set up a time to talk with the person, not in your imagination but face-to-face. When you sit down together, make your intention clear. It will build cooperation if the other person knows what benefits you hope both of you can derive from this discussion. "I want to be able to have a closer relationship with you, but these are the issues that get in my way. . . . It's out of my love for you and my hopes for a healthier relationship that I'm talking to you now." Then, focus on one event or issue, covering the following three important points:

1. This is what happened.
2. This is how I felt about it at the time.
3. This is what I want from you now.

Ask the person merely to listen to all three points without responding, agreeing, or disagreeing. With no criticism or blame, state the issue, trying to be as clear, brief, and specific as possible. Speak about your own experience and feelings, using as many "I" statements as you can.

Then ask the person to reflect on what you've said to make sure your message has come across accurately and clearly.

It is important to understand that such discussions can indeed create breakthroughs, but that substantial changes in a relationship must come out of thoughtful assessment followed by small steps and clear and consistent statements and actions. One talk will not necessarily create lasting change; consistent action will. In that vein, when she felt clear about the issues she wanted to discuss with her mother, Liana had several talks with her mother using the format described above. She was able to communicate these concerns without blaming or intimidating her mother.

In our talks, we were able to discuss the issues in our relationship that had been bothering me, particularly ones from my childhood. As we talked openly with each other, I began to see her as a person, not just as my mother. I realize now how much I kept her in the role of a mother. Since she constantly fell short of my ideal mother, I felt resentment and anger toward her for not being perfect. Once I was able to see her as a human being who had gone through her own struggles and had grown up along with us as a mother, we had some interesting conversations about her marriage, the status of women at the time of my childhood, and how these larger social issues affected her mothering. I was able to see my mother as a human being, and this helped me have compassion and understanding for her. We share our human struggles, not just our struggles as mother and daughter.

Carl Jung once wrote that until we see our parents as people with their own wounds, limitations, and failures, we are unable to grow up. When we can forgive our parents as human beings, then we can release the past and accept our parents without trying to change them. Liana discovered that this new understanding and compassion for her mother brought about a deeper and more functional relationship between them.

Many find that part of the healing of the relationship with a living parent involves separating expectations and inevitable disappointments from reality. Deep inside each of us, we hold an image of who we want our parents to be; these images often have an archetypal origin. A flesh-and-blood parent can never measure up to these images, but our expectations and hopes often blind us to that reality. In beginning to acknowledge the relationship as it is, we can come to appreciate what our parents have given us and to accept what they haven't.

By the way, if your family member is unwilling to accept your invitation to talk, consider writing a letter. This can be a nonthreatening way to reach out, giving the recipient time to absorb the contents without the pressure to respond immediately. Meanwhile, by continuing to work with internal communication, you may be able to influence the person's receptivity to talking, and this work can help you make peace with the relationship as it is.

EXERCISE 3

When a Family Member Is Dying

New responsibilities and roles often rise up within a family when one member begins to die. As a result, resentments can surface about contributions of time, energy, and money. Regular family meetings can be useful throughout the illness and periodically during the months of grief to discuss and work out issues, divide up responsibilities, and explore new roles with one another. This exercise will help to keep channels of communication clear.

Set a regular time for meeting, and appoint one person, preferably a different person each time, to be a timekeeper and to help keep the discussion on track.

Use a "talking stick"—a stick, stone, flower, or other object—passing it to each person in turn. Whoever holds the stick may speak without being interrupted while the others listen with full attention. In this way, each person updates the rest on what he or she has been going through since the last meeting.

Follow up on issues that were discussed in the last meeting. Which decisions were implemented, and which were not? Are there still some unresolved feelings about issues that were discussed?

Write down current issues of concern.

Brainstorm possible solutions and strategies. In this phase, it is important not to edit or judge any ideas. Write them all down.

Agree on one strategy for each issue and divide up responsibilities among family members for carrying out tasks.

Go around the circle so that each person can express appreciation or admiration for each of the other family members present.

Set a date for the next meeting. Then close the meeting with a prayer, blessing, poem, or song. Family members can take turns bringing an idea for closing the meeting.

Since the dying of a family member puts considerable stress on the family, disagreements and fights are common, though often unexpected. When outer communication breaks down, you can use your imagination to meet the dying person in a healing place and talk about the issues that have been troubling the relationship. Internal communication techniques can help you work through difficult issues and heal old hurts. As you strengthen your imagination, you will increase your capacity to put yourself into the thoughts and feelings of others, thereby promoting compassion and respect for differences and fostering clear and effective external communication within the family.

CHAPTER 8

Reaching Your Living Partner

The illness and dying of a family member can put tremendous strain on a marriage or partnership, making new demands of time, attention, and money. While one partner is attending to the dying person, the other partner may well feel abandoned and left out. In response, the partner making the effort and doing the work may feel unsupported and misunderstood.

When the person dies, though the partners expect relief of the tensions on their marriage, they may find a whole new set in place. As I have shown, grieving is an intensely emotional and unstable time. Exhausted after a prolonged period of caring for a dying parent in the family, the adult child may now have the additional stress of caring for survivors, who are also grieving. There is often little energy left over for a partner.

Furthermore, the "outsider" may feel overwhelmed by the intensity of the other's grief. Particularly if he or she has not yet experienced the death of a family member, this person may just not understand the intensity of the experience. The nongrieving partner may see confusing, even alarming, and rapid changes in the grieving partner and ask, "Who *is* this person? This seems like a stranger, not the person I married at all." Nevertheless, changes in one partner will necessitate changes in the relationship, whether or not the other partner is willing to make them. Understandably, the need to work at change can trigger resentment of the other partner.

Moreover, partners may deal with such stresses differently, owing to cultural differences, family conditioning, and birth order. So the effects of the death spiral on and on, and disagreements are common.

More often than not, however, in the midst of their family loss, couples tend to downplay the extent of the stress it places on their partnership. They may not even recognize that the escalation of fights or tension has its underlying source in grief. This is particularly true in the months of grief after the immediate crisis of the illness and dying has passed. At that time, those in grief often feel pressure from partners, friends, and other family members to snap out of it and get on with their lives. Yet the grieving process goes on and on, shaking up partnerships and initiating intensive change.

Surviving Turbulence

In response to the changes in the grieving person, many partners in intimate relationships can expect to go through a period of turbulence. Just as in other areas of life during this time, issues that have been simmering under the surface may come up; compromises that have been tolerated for years may suddenly become intolerable. Both partners might see unhealthy patterns in the relationship with increased clarity, and particularly the grieving partner may be less likely to tolerate these patterns than before. Some marriages and partnerships grow apart and split up under these new pressures. Many of my clients have confirmed that their partners' lack of support through such a major and difficult life event had been a major factor in their decision to terminate a marriage or relationship.

If a marriage or partnership is going to survive this difficult time, communication is critical. As with Liana and her husband, many couples find that, at the very time they most need to, they are unable to talk with one another in a meaningful and supportive way. At the beginning of a relationship, most partners feel that they can talk with their mates freely and honestly. However, over time, hurts and misunderstandings accumulate; unrealistic expectations produce disappointments. With so much at stake, partners tend to hide their vulnerability and needs, mask their anger, and avoid discussions of sensitive issues. Unexpressed feelings then find expression in distorted ways; for example, in explosions of anger, repetitious arguments, and sarcastic and belittling comments. This breakdown in communication becomes critical when one or both partners are grieving and desperately need the other person's understanding and support.

Internal communication techniques can be highly effective in breaking through damaging patterns of communication and working through old hurts that are currently affecting the relationship. The imagery exercises in chapter 4 are useful in this context; also, letter-writing—you write to your partner and create a response, all without sending the letters—is a nonconfrontational way of working through difficult feelings. I recommend using the format that John Gray describes in *Men Are from Mars, Women Are from Venus*. He suggests first writing a love letter that expresses your feelings of love as well as anger, sadness, and regret about the relationship. Write it as though your partner were open to hearing what you have to say. Next, write a response letter, a reply from your partner's point of view. Include in this letter whatever you wish to hear from your partner in the way of acknowledgment, understanding, and support. Writing these letters will give you the opportunity to express what you think, feel, and want. You'll also learn to listen to yourself, since you'll be writing a letter of acknowledgment back to yourself. Once you are able not only to express yourself openly and honestly but also to honor that expression, you will be much more likely to feel yourself heard and supported by your partner. Although the exercise does not require it, you may indeed decide to share these letters with your partner to help him or her better understand your needs.

Once you have voiced unexpressed feelings and gained more understanding and compassion, then an actual exchange of letters between partners may be helpful in rebuilding trust and intimacy. Writing and actually delivering letters to one another can help each partner explore and express feelings and concerns in a safe way. Receiving letters can help each partner take in and reflect on the concerns of the other without the pressure of having to respond immediately. This gives a partner necessary feedback and shows where change is needed. Then each partner can read and reflect on what has been written, learn what is important to the other, and decide what he or she can do to support the other person.

The following exercise is for both partners.

EXERCISE 1

A Grief Letter

Write a letter to your partner, focusing on how grief has affected and changed your partnership. Go into separate rooms and write your letters, being as honest and open as you can. Focus on your feelings and concerns. If you are the grieving partner, write about your experience of grieving: What has been difficult for you? What are your fears? What have you appreciated about your partner? What have you resented or regretted? What do you want from your partner? Do you feel your partner has supported you? If not, what could he or she do to better support you? Have any new realizations or understandings come out of your grief? What patterns in your relationship do you see more clearly now? What changes do you want to make in your relationship?

If you are the nongrieving partner, write about how it has been for you to live with a person who is grieving: What has been difficult or challenging for you? How have you felt about the changes you've seen in your partner? Have you felt left out or abandoned? Have you felt appreciated for your efforts to support your partner through this crisis? What do you now appreciate, fear, or regret? What do you want from your partner? What are your visions of the future?

In both cases, write as though your partner were listening with love and understanding. Take the risk of sharing feelings and thoughts that you ordinarily hold back. Try to focus on your own experience rather than blaming or judging your partner.

When you've both finished your letters, exchange them. Take your time to read your partner's letter, reflecting on what has been expressed. You can either write a response or sit down together to talk about your responses.

Once you have written letters in this manner, assess your readiness to talk with your partner, as you did with members of your family of origin:

- Am I able to speak out truthfully as well as listen respectfully?
- Am I able to understand the other person's point of view?
- Do I still feel upset about the issues I addressed in my letter?
- Am I clear about what I want in my relationship?

Six months after the death of Liana's father, Liana and Tim's marriage was suffering from a year of neglect, lack of communication, and tumultuous emotions. The year before her father had died, Liana had been frequently away from home, caring for him. Even though he understood her concerns for her father, Tim felt pushed away and abandoned. His hopes that their marriage would return to normal after the death were not realized; her grief seemed to go on and on and the intensity of it was often overwhelming to him. Liana, on the other hand, felt lonely and unsupported. Every time she tried to talk to Tim about her concerns, the discussion ended up in a fight; neither person felt understood or heard. In an effort to establish communication again, Liana and Tim agreed to write letters to one another.

DEAR TIM,

These last few months have been so hard for me. I've felt alone and overwhelmed. My father's death hit me harder than I ever would have expected. Out of this pain, I've been forced to question so much in my life that I'd previously taken for granted—including our marriage. It's become so clear to me how much our communication has broken down. In the past few years we've talked about our children, our bills, and our jobs, but we've avoided talking about how we feel about each other. Now we avoid talking about my grief.

I've wanted your support. I've never felt so alone and confused. And yet whenever I've tried to talk to you about what I'm feeling, you seemed uncomfortable and distracted. I resent that your business gets so much of your time and attention and I get so little. I remember feeling this same way as a teenager when I tried talking with my father.

I need you to listen to me—about what I'm feeling, about the changes that I've experienced since my father's death, about the frustrations I feel in our marriage. I know that you may not understand what I'm going through, but I want you to at least try to. I've felt so alone when I'm with you. I want to feel close to you again!

DEAR LIANA,

You've seemed so distant lately. I often ask myself: "Where is the woman I married?" You used to be so optimistic, so cheerful. This change in you has disappointed me and confused me. Our marriage is different. Everything feels somber and heavy now. I've felt helpless watching you go through such a hard time after your father's death. I haven't known how to help or make you feel better. I have felt some pressure to do something, but I haven't known what to do or say. In some way, I feel that I've failed you. I need to know how I can support you, help you. I need to know that you still care about me.

After exchanging these letters, Tim and Liana felt more understanding. Tim learned that all he had to do was listen. It was a revelation to him that he didn't have to make his wife feel better. After writing her letter, Liana realized that she had experienced the same feelings of abandonment with her father that she now felt with her husband. This made her wonder whether some of her current anger and disappointment wasn't a carryover from her relationship with her father in adolescence. To explore this possibility further, Liana decided to work on her relationship with her father using internal communication (see chapter 4). A few weeks later, Tim and Liana felt ready to sit down and talk with one another about the issues they had previously avoided. This time, each of them was able to speak about current concerns in their relationship and to listen to the other respectfully.

Weekly talks are an important part of the grieving period: talks in which each person can voice concerns, resentments, appreciations, discuss what is and isn't working, and explore solutions. Such talks can build intimacy and provide the space for partners to explore creative solutions to new demands and problems. They also keep resentments from building up. In *The New Peoplemaking*, Virginia Satir wrote, "Once a human being has arrived on this earth, communication is the largest single factor determining what kinds of relationships she or he makes with others and what happens to each in the world" (Satir, p. 51).

With the death of a loved one, many issues regarding life's meaning may suddenly intrude themselves into daily life: what you must do to die in peace, what gives purpose and meaning to life, what hopes, fears, and dreams you harbor, what it means to live fully and authentically, how you are related to the infinite. The philosopher Friedrich Nietzsche called marriage a grand conversation (Nietzsche, p. 59). Although a loss puts tremendous stress on a partnership, often in a sudden and unexpected way, confronting and responding to this major crisis allows a dialogue to open that can renew and deepen the relationship and enrich both partners.

A HEALING DIALOGUE

Chris and Rebecca talked incessantly of issues of meaning and loss as they both grieved the death of their fathers. Both fathers died suddenly of heart attacks, Rebecca's two years before Chris's. As is often the case, the first death was the most difficult for their marriage, because Chris did not really understand what Rebecca was going through. With the second death, their shared experience of loss drew them closer and helped resolve the earlier misunderstandings. The dialogue that continued over the months enriched their relationship and helped them both mature as marriage partners. Here is their account to me of this deep and productive inner change.

REBECCA: After my father died, Chris was very supportive, but I felt very alone. It was the first time we went to marriage counseling. It was hard that he couldn't understand why I needed him. Just recently, we talked about this, and I asked him if, since his own father's death, he now understood more what I was talking about then. He said yes. Until you've experienced it, you just don't know.

CHRIS: With our parents' passing, we are more capable of looking at how we want to be together. It's given me a much clearer idea of how I want to be right now and how I want to be in the future. I didn't use to think about the future with Rebecca as much. Day to day was fine. I've always used the day-at-a-time method for keeping commitment and devotion. Now the quality has changed.

I've gone through two major events of my life with Rebecca: my father's death and sobriety. I don't know what it would have been like to do these two things without her. In my worst moments, I'll think I couldn't have done it without her, but in my better moments, I think I'm lucky and fortunate that I did have someone to help me through these things.

REBECCA: It bonded us even more.

In supporting one another through the death of their fathers, Rebecca and Chris realized that their marriage was an important and creative collaboration for moving through major life transitions. They came to see their marriage in a new context, with new responsibilities.

CHRIS: It was moving-up day. I realized at that moment that we weren't kids anymore. We were now our parents' generation. Becoming the generation that's in the middle, that takes care of the older and the younger people, broke a barrier for me. When her father died, I understood for the first time one of the reasons people have children. I suddenly realized what it would be like to be alone.

Chris and Rebecca both appreciated the fact that, in the face of the devastating loss of a parent, the companionship and support of a partner are priceless. They each expressed faith in their partner's ability to come through for them in the future. Every spouse wonders whether the partner will really be there at a time of great crisis, and the death of a parent can be the first major test of this question. If a partner does pass this test, a great infusion of confidence in the relationship can help both people move through the challenges and losses of midlife.

THE POSITIVE IMPACT OF A DEATH

After the death of a loved one, partners are likely to take marriage much more seriously. They realize in a concrete way that time is limited, life is precious, and love is more important than anything else. With this awareness, many people have set out to challenge the conditioning that holds them back from the loving and supportive relationships that they want and deserve.

The death of Robin's parents impelled her to reevaluate her understanding of marriage and relationship—versions that she had inherited from her parents.

It wasn't just burying these two individuals who raised me and protected me and had been there every breathing minute that I had walked this earth. I buried my childhood, I buried all sense of a connection to human beings that had any history on me. I also buried my parents' marriage. My parents' deaths helped me see who my parents were as individuals: how they related to one another, how my mother saw herself as a woman, how my father saw her as a woman. I began to clarify what concepts I inherited from them and what were really my own.

As Robin's comments demonstrate, the death of a parent can dramatically increase awareness of parental conditioning and its effect on one's own marriage. Parental expectations, as well as the difficulties and patterns in a parents' relationship, can unconsciously and insidiously affect the formation of similar patterns in one's own marriage or intimate relationship. It can be a rude shock to wake up and see clearly how much like one's parents one has become, despite efforts to move in the opposite direction. The definitive separation from a parent through death can free the adult child to challenge the conditioning that may have set a blueprint for relationships.

The time of a parent's death can be a fertile time for gathering and assessing information about your family history from your surviving parent and other relatives. In doing this, you may become aware of certain themes or patterns that thread through the generations. Do you see patterns in your parents' relationship that are similar to those in your own marriage or intimate relationship? Did your grandparents or great-grandparents struggle with the same issues you face now? Do you want to continue these patterns in your own life?

Family patterns get passed down until one family member stops to ask, "Is this actually appropriate or healthy for me? Is this what I really want in my life or my relationships?"

Use internal communication to explore patterns and conditioning that have affected each generation. Write a letter to a deceased family member, expressing your concern about issues that he or she had struggled with and that you find yourself facing today. You can also write your family member's response.

Serafina saw a disturbing pattern of sexual oppression affecting the women of her maternal lineage. As a mother of two daughters, she felt impelled to break the cycle. In a letter, she turned to her grandmother for guidance, advice, and support. Her grandmother's love had sustained her through her childhood, and she felt it would help her now face a shameful family issue.

Dear Grandma,

As I start this letter, tears well up in my eyes and my chest muscles tighten. I miss you so much. You were so soft and kind in a world of pain and confusion. When it felt like my whole family was against me, you lovingly took me into your arms. You alone saw me as special.

Being in your presence was like a gift from God. I felt safe and loved. I have to admit though, Grandma, I didn't like Grandpa too much. He scared me. He seemed mean and ornery and always held on to us too long and too tight when he hugged us. I feel ashamed to admit this, but I felt kind of glad when he died. It's funny, nobody else seemed too heartbroken, either. I don't remember my mother crying.

I loved the big green and white house you lived in. It was always a mystery to me. I often wondered what went on inside this three-story house with seven children. What did you think of Grandpa as a husband/father? I wish you could tell me some stories about my mother.

The upstairs is where my mother's bedroom was. She did not seem to like visiting her old room, nor did I. How come? What happened? Mom says she has some vague memories of being sexually molested by Grandpa. Were you ever molested? How come your mother, who lived right across the street, wouldn't talk to you? I heard she didn't like Grandpa. Is that true? How come she didn't like Grandpa?

After Grandpa died, your energy became lighter. Even so, there was a sadness in your chocolate brown eyes. A sadness that spoke of eons of oppression. I know it sounds weird, but I feel like you and my entire maternal ancestry are counting on me to end the oppression. This is so hard. When you died, I felt so all alone, like a safety net had been pulled out from underneath me. I was only fourteen years old and a victim of oppression myself.

Grandma, I just want you to know that I am fighting back. I will change the history of our lineage. I have two daughters of my own now, and it is up to me to break the cycle. I will not allow the oppression to continue one generation longer. Your sadness is my strength. I know you are with me, guiding me, cheering me on, and loving me.

About a year ago, I felt your presence so strongly that I felt moved to erect a shrine in your memory. Since your death, I have undergone many changes. I married at age twenty and had two daughters shortly thereafter. Unlike everyone else in the family, I've managed to go to college and am currently working on my master's degree. Difficult as it was and will continue to be, I have gained a sense of freedom from the oppression that has plagued the women of this family for centuries. I hope you can feel it, too. I can now accept your death as part of the ongoing cycle of life, and although I miss you very much, I know that things are as they should be.

WITH LOVE AND GRATITUDE,
SERAFINA

Connecting with her grandmother through this letter helped Serafina tap her own inner strength. She felt resolved to be the instrument of change in her family system: "I will not allow the oppression to continue one generation longer. Your sadness is my strength. I know you are with me, guiding me, cheering me on, and loving me."

Ray, whose letter to her father appears earlier, observed that she was living out the relationship with her partner in the same way that her father had lived with her mother:

My father's death made me realize that I had been living out my relationship with my partner exactly as he lived out his relationship with my mother: don't rock the boat, just live your life side by side, but don't ever ask or expect anything. Both of our partners were obsessed with their own work.

Becoming aware of dysfunctional family patterns can be painful, but such pain can be a powerful motivation to change. When we set about creating change, there can be strong resistance not only from within the family but also from within the self. It can feel terrifying and lonely to break out of a pattern that is deeply entrenched in the family history. However, the death of a loved one can provide just the momentum needed to break through this inevitable resistance.

As you deepen and transform your relationship with a partner through communication—both internal and external—you may discover that an intimate partnership is not just a coming together of two individuals but the mysterious formation of a third entity, one that is greater than either individual can be separately and that invites you both to grow and expand beyond your individual limitations.

CHAPTER 9

Reaching Your Living Children

The loss of a loved one can deepen parents' appreciation of their children, even when they consider it impossible to cherish the children more than they do. Many parents who experience a loss not only value their time with their children more afterward but also feel a new urgency about improving the quality of their parenting. One of my clients told me that six months after the death of his mother, "my relationships with my children are so much more important to me.... Now that I realize how quickly my time with them will pass, I feel a strong commitment to spending more quality time with them, expressing my appreciation of them as individuals and healing the wounds I have created in our relationship through my own conditioning and negligence. I have been looking at all the ways I have parented them that have divided us rather than brought us closer."

A bereavement period, then, can be a time when one takes parenting into one's own hands. Looking at how their parenting has been influenced by their own parents' advice and agendas, parents can begin to define parenting from their own values and standards.

Letting Go

Parenting involves a delicate dance of close connection and separation. In reaction to the loss of a family member, we may tend to hold on tighter to our children. However, as we let go of a deceased loved one, we must also learn to let our children go. Remembering our own struggles to separate from our parents, we can appreciate our children's struggle to separate from us. We must let go of them so they can be themselves.

Natural developments aid in the letting-go process. The loss of a family member can help us see and honor a child as an individual rather than as an extension of ourselves or of our family. Many parents unconsciously live out their own ambitions and dreams through their children. It was for this reason that Carl Jung wrote that the unlived life of the parent was the child's greatest burden. However, the awakening to one's own life that typically occurs after the loss of a parent can actually free children to be themselves and explore their own unique paths.

Consider Jacqueline, who struggled with the spirited nature of her daughter from the moment the girl was born. Jacqueline herself had been conditioned to be "a nice girl," and she unconsciously expected her very feisty daughter to conform to the rules as well. But when her mother died, Jacqueline felt freed to explore her own feistiness, and as a result came to respect and honor this quality in her daughter. This changed her relationship with her daughter. Suddenly, she could relax and enjoy her.

The whole constellation moves in a different way. My parents' myth of being nice—not asking too much, hoping for the best, and then secretly fuming if you don't get it—has shifted. Now there's open space for that story to be rewritten. Being nice is not one of my daughter's struggles, never was and never will

be. My mother tried to tame my spirit. I wasn't a nice little girl
with bows in my hair, and I couldn't be. Neither is my daughter. I can actualize my daughter's strength so much more.

INTEGRATING THE TRUTH

Just as a death in the family can affect a parent's perception
of his or her child, so it can alter a child's perspective on life
and death. When this happens, it is important for the parent/
child relationship to serve as a sanctuary for the child, where
he or she can explore and integrate new awarenesses. As
children watch a family member die or a parent grieve, they
may feel frightened at the prospect of other family members
dying. One four-year-old who witnessed both her father's
death and that of a family friend asked, "Why are there so
many deaths? Am I going to die? Are you?" It is important
to listen to your children's concerns and to take time to explore their questions.

A child's first exposure to death is often accompanied by
a period of moodiness and instability while the child struggles to integrate the awareness that loved ones do in fact die.
In the months after my father's death, my six-year-old son
and I had many talks at bedtime about his concerns about
death. Some of his questions were hard for me to face; for
example, "What will happen to me when you die? Who will
take care of me? Can't I die before you?" His tears pulled
at my heart. But in acknowledging his fears, exploring his
questions, and embracing the mystery of death along with
my son, I could see a deeper appreciation for the precious-
ness of life develop within him. And I saw subtle signs that
he was beginning to accept death as a natural part of the life
cycle. After a book-signing party for *Losing a Parent*, he
threw his arms around me and told me with great confidence
and enthusiasm, "Mama, you'll be so proud of me. When
you die, I'll write *Losing a Parent Part II*!" I was a bit taken

aback but pleasantly surprised. The awareness of the fragility of life and the certainty of death can make parents appreciate the relationship with their children—and children with their parents—even more than before.

Young children often have difficulty expressing to their parents what it is that troubles them about the death of someone close to them. The following exercise gives children the opportunity to confront their problems in symbolic language and to gain help and guidance from their imaginations. They can express their feelings and concerns to the people and animals they meet in their imaginations, dialogue with them, and learn new ways of coping from them.

EXERCISE 1

Writing a Fairy Tale

Create a stack of index cards with the names of places, magical beings, magical objects, people, and animals listed below (see the groupings below for suggestions). Then place these cards face down in stacks, one for each category. Choose a time, such as bedtime, and create an environment that is conducive to storytelling. Ensure that you will not be interrupted. Close the door, light a candle, gather special toys around the bed. Invite your child to choose one card randomly from each of the five stacks. Reading each one out loud, lay the chosen cards before you both.

Ask your child to start with the magical opening, "Once upon a time," and tell you a fairy tale that features these five words. Encourage your child to use the words in any order and to add any other words desired. If your child expresses doubts about being able to create a fairy tale, assure him or her that the fairy tale, once started, will soon begin to tell itself.

An older child may choose to write the fairy tale

rather than tell it out loud. Then one of you can read it out loud to the other.

When the fairy tale is finished, ask your child to give it a title. Your child can also illustrate the fairy tale and then create a small book.

Take some time to reflect on your child's fairy tale. What is the central challenge or test in the story? What form did help or guidance take? How does the central character overcome adversity, and how is that character strengthened by these ordeals? Does the fairy tale reflect your child's inner conflicts or anxieties? Does the fairy tale inspire new perspectives and insights? Did you observe any changes in your child after creating the fairy tale? If so, what changes? How can you support any growth or new perspectives that your child's fairy tale inspired?

Places: Mountain, bazaar, sea, valley, pool, lake, desert, castle, mountain pass, village, cave, tunnel, meadow, tree, garden, forest, fire, dungeon, church, bridge, city, crossroads, fountain, hollow, island, palace, river, ship, temple, tower, volcano, wall, door, house, spring

Animals and Other Creatures: Turtle, raven, worm, serpent, dove, whale, horse, fish, sparrow, crane, camel, lamb, rat, owl, frog, swan, fox, crocodile, dog, cat, swallow, bear, lion, eagle, monkey, bee, pig, dolphin, peacock, ox, hare, lion, cock, wolf, bull, butterfly, crow, dove, elephant, leopard, spider, stag, vulture, hawk

Magical Beings: Unicorn, dragon, troll, giant, fairy, goblin, mermaid, angel, sorceress, dwarf, monster, wizard, soothsayer, fairy godmother, phoenix, centaur, griffin, trickster, shaman

Magical Objects: Egg, gold, cauldron, ring, ivory, stone, crown, shell, cross, treasure, seed, chalice, drum, star, horn, anchor, pearl, bell, arrow, ladder, sword, rose, book, ax, bone, bow, candle, cloak, crystal, diamond, feather, fire, flute, goblet, chalice, grail, helmet, herbs, jewel, key, lamp, lyre, mask, mirror, pearl, rope, veil, trident, thunderbolt, torch, thorn, moon, sun, thread

People: Harpist, hermit, knight, princess, prince, queen, king, mother, father, grandmother, grandfather, musician, old man, old woman, harlot, wild man, child, clown, farmer, priest, priestess, nun, monk, maiden, carpenter, healer, girl, boy, pirate, gypsy, fool, brother, sister, virgin, twin, invalid, friend, orphan, crone

---

Fairy tales are healing to both adults and children. In *The Uses of Enchantment*, Bruno Bettelheim wrote, "Each fairy tale is a magic mirror which reflects some aspects of our inner world.... For those who immerse themselves in what the fairy tale has to communicate, it becomes a deep, quiet pool which at first seems to reflect only our own image; but behind it we soon discover the inner turmoils of our soul—its depth, and ways to gain peace within ourselves and with the world, which is the reward of our struggles" (Bettleheim, p. 309). The people of fairy tales confront suffering, hardship, trials, isolation, abandonment, and loss. Each person finds help and guidance; each finds a way through the ordeals, attaining love, happiness, wisdom, or riches. Fairy tales assure us that when we struggle against the inevitable difficulties of life such as the loss of a loved one, we can turn to the imagination for the resources we need to heal and go on with our lives.

Fairy tales teach us that in the imagination, things are often other than what they seem: a kind grandmother may be a hungry wolf, an ugly frog may be a charming prince, a gift may be a curse. Even death may not be the ending we take it to be. In many fairy tales, death is not the end of the story or the end of a life. A person can be dead at one point in the story and then restored to life at a later one. Snow White's death is mourned by those who love her, but she comes back to life, even more beautiful than she had been. Little Red Riding Hood leaps out of the wolf's belly, transformed into a mature maiden. In reading and rereading fairy tales, we learn to prepare ourselves for the new beginnings, unexpected events, and transformations hidden within death.

By focusing on the interaction between two brothers in his fairy tale, a six-year-old I'll call Casey was able to express and explore his feelings about the death of his older brother, which had occurred nine months before. Casey's imagination guided him right to the source of his unresolved grief—the guilt and anger that had been festering inside him for months. Since he had avoided talking about his brother's death, the fairy tale represented a breakthrough for both Casey and his mother. By reading his fairy tale, his mother was able to discover how her son was dealing with his loss. This child picked these words: fountain, monster, cauldron, twins, and dove. With his mother writing it down, he then created the following story.

BROTHERLY LOVE

Once upon a time, in a land far, far away, there was a town. In the center of the town was a fountain. Underneath the **fountain**, there lived a **monster** who only ate children and loved to eat **twins**.

In the town there was only one set of twins, John and Danny. John was the smart one, and Danny was the strong one. Now this monster was always trying to get the twins to stand over the trap door that led to his home.

One day, when John was sick, their mom sent Danny out for some medicine. Without John to warn him, Danny stood right on top of the trap door. The monster cooked him in a big **cauldron** and ate him.

When John heard of Danny's death, he asked a little **dove** to help him kill the monster. So, one day, with the dove at his side, John stood above the trap door. When the monster captured him, he told the dove to fly around the monster's head fast. When the dove was finished, the monster was so dizzy that he fell backward into the cauldron and died.

But John's life wasn't full. He still missed Danny. One night a spirit came down from the heavens and said, "If you keep him alive in your heart, he will never die."

The End

In the opening lines of his fairy tale, Casey gives death a form he can relate to: a monster who traps and eats twin brothers. Casey then carefully delineates the revenge that brother John exacts on the monster. Although Casey had probably felt helpless watching his sick brother die, John was not powerless; he plotted a way to trick the monster and then kill him. This healing story helps Casey relive the trauma of losing his brother, express his rage toward a tangible object, and discover that his brother lives on in his heart, where he will never die.

CHAPTER 10

Reaching Living Friends

Friendships often change in quality and intensity—even quantity—after a loved one's death. With new priorities and clarified values, people who have lost someone significant to them often come to appreciate the importance of their friendships anew and come to take more responsibility for their quality. This can result in the deepening of some friendships and the letting go of others. As a family shrinks with the death of one or both parents, grandparents, and siblings, the members begin to redefine their sense of family, expanding it to embrace friends or mentors. A new appreciation may develop, too, for a living sense of community. Robin describes just such an experience.

After my parents died, my relationships started changing with women and men. I dropped the unhealthy ones, while others grew healthier and deeper. I began to choose my friends more consciously. Subsequently, I think I have quite an array of friends. I've never felt more loved in my entire life. I read a quote a while ago that said, "In the evening of our lives we will be judged on love alone." I feel so lucky that in the broad daylight of my life I know exactly what that person is saying, and love is the most important thing. I feel so much more capable of loving, not just other people, but myself.

Shifting Sands

Although a few friends might come forward with support and understanding during a time of loss, it is also common for some to back away at this critical time, intimidated by changes in grieving friends' behavior or uncomfortable with the intensity of emotions. It's not unusual for people to report that a death in the family shows who a person's real friends are.

Like Robin, Jacqueline became more discerning in the quality of her friendships after her parents died. In contrast to Robin, she felt less inclined to spend time with her friends than before, choosing instead to spend more time with her family and by herself. This was a marked change in her life, as she had previously given priority to her friends. She told me, "I don't have the patience or the energy to go through friendships that are compromised. I'd much rather be alone than talk about superficial things."

In experiencing such shifts and changes in what you want from your friendships, it is helpful to speak out directly to let your friends know what isn't working for you—and, of course, what is. Too many people mistakenly assume that their friends perceive the friendship just as they do, and this unrecognized lack of congruence can lead to misunderstandings. Friendships that survive will go through inevitable adjustments. My friend Eileen moved to Europe a few months before I heard that my father had cancer. In the chaotic months that followed, I reached out to her, but she was absorbed in helping her family adjust to a new home. No matter how hard I tried to explain to her what I was going through, she seemed unable to understand. Finally, out of desperation, I wrote and expressed my anger at her neglect at such a critical time for me. She called me immediately from Germany, and from that point became much more responsive. Not having experienced the dying of a parent herself, she had had no idea what this was like. To give the support and understanding we hope for from them, friends need to be educated about the impact of death and dying within a family.

While critical issues may surface in a friendship after the death of a loved one, a person in grief may feel too overwhelmed to explore these issues in person. In such cases, internal communication can help take the pressure off and provide some sense of resolution until the person feels ready to communicate outwardly.

Sometimes, the person who has lost a loved one feels too raw and vulnerable to risk rejection. One of my clients, Gloria, told me that after her mother's death, she stopped reaching out to her friends and stopped returning their calls, a dramatic change in her behavior. Also, she felt lonely and disturbed by the fights that were erupting with her partner. Whereas before her mother's death she had had a broad support network, in her grief she turned solely to her partner for support and comfort. This placed enormous pressure on that single relationship; hence, the fights.

As we explored this situation together, Gloria discovered that she had made assumptions about friendship that now closed off her options. She believed that it was only fair that she listen equally to her friends' concerns and problems if she was going to share hers. As a result, she didn't call her friends in her grief because she lacked the energy in her grief to listen to her friends' problems. We talked about the possibility of sharing this dilemma with her friends rather than withdrawing from them. It is always critical to keep from making assumptions about what a friend wants or expects, assumptions that can hold friendships to old molds at a time when so much opportunity exists for renewal and change.

As Gloria reviewed her friendships, she identified a couple of people whom she wanted to contact. Others she chose not to contact because she wasn't sure she wanted these friendships to continue. In these cases, she chose to use internal communication exercises in my office to express her anger and disappointment in their reactions to her grief. Working through old hurts in this way helped her feel more at peace. As they watch their loved ones die, many people come to realize in a new and concrete way just how important friends and family are, understanding that they want love in their lives and don't want to die in loneliness.

Ray explains how her father's lonely death made her want to deepen her friendships by sharing more meaningful experiences with them.

Even though we were there touching him and taking care of him, my father still had a lonely death, because he had been lonely his whole life. I don't want that to happen to me, and I recognize a very profound loneliness in myself.

I have my deep experiences alone, then I tell my friends. I don't have deep, meaningful experiences with them. So that's another safety valve I have. I think this involves my lack of trust. My father told me, "Nobody likes you. They only pretend to like you." That was his own projection. I think it really did affect me. I'm always waiting for somebody to pull out on me.

As in Ray's experience, our relationships with others can be affected unconsciously by our parents' comments, projections, and unspoken judgments. After the death of a loved one, when our new clarity allows us to see so much of ourselves anew, we may begin to recognize such projections and challenge their power over us.

To summarize, then, the death of a loved one within the family can make or break a friendship. Note how Robin, Ray, and Gloria began to take their friendships more seriously. All three accepted responsibility for deepening the potentially enriching friendships while dropping those they came to identify as draining and unfulfilling. These three join many others in realizing that the experience of losing a loved one has made them better friends with an increased capacity for compassion, honesty, and understanding.

COMMUNICATING WITH FRIENDS

Since communication with friends can be difficult or strained while you are grieving, it is helpful to have several communication options. If it becomes difficult to talk to your friend, try writing a letter. If that doesn't work for you, internal communication techniques can help you deal with sensitive issues, express your feelings, and gain an understanding of the other person's position. For example, you might want to use your imagination to meet your friend in a healing place or carry on an internal dialogue.

Let your friends know what you want and need from them. Offer them some suggestions of ways they can help and support you—perhaps by bringing you a meal, doing some errands, giving you a back rub, taking a walk with you, checking in on you regularly. Make it clear that you need to withdraw (if you do). Encourage your friends to educate themselves about grief so that they will know what to expect. Remind them that grief takes a long time to heal.

If you feel too vulnerable or overwhelmed to have a conversation, write your friend a letter, stating what you need and want as well as what your friendship means to you. Identify anything the friend is doing that runs counter to your needs. For example, your friend may be avoiding talking about your grief, even though you want to.

If you don't want to communicate but need to work on some unresolved issues in the relationship, use internal communication techniques, particularly exercise 1, An Internal Encounter, in chapter 7.

When you feel ready, talk with your friend. Refer to exercise 2, An External Encounter, in chapter 7. Prepare carefully by thinking through your concerns ahead of time as you can identify and address any changes that may have occurred in your friendship as a result of your grieving.

Suggestions for Friends

To better support your grieving friend, remember that using internal communication techniques will help you maintain a connection with your friend, even if he or she has withdrawn from you. You can work with imagery to meet your friend in an imaginal world, write a letter, or create a dialogue. The following suggestions will also help you integrate grief into your friendship day to day.

Educate yourself about what your grieving friend is going through. Read books on grief, listen to tapes, talk with others who have grieved. You can expect your grieving friend to be emotional, raw, restless, and unpredictable. Don't expect normalcy too soon. Your friend may want to be with you sometimes and alone at others. He or she may want to talk sometimes and remain silent with you at others. Take your friend's lead.

It is important to acknowledge the death and the impact this has had on your friend. Recognize that your friend is in an altered state. Understand, if you can, that moods will shift abruptly and that simple contact can be greatly soothing. Express interest in your friend's feelings and concerns. Remember that you don't have to make your friend feel better. If your friend cries, be as supportive as you can. If your friend needs to talk, listen. Be trustworthy with confidences. Avoid giving lots of advice, even though you feel impelled to do this because you feel helpless in the face of so much pain.

Help in small ways. You can bring meals and flowers, offer to do errands, send cards, and check in regularly by phone.

Be willing to admit your helplessness in the situation and

be honest if you feel overwhelmed or frightened by the intensity of your friend's feelings. You may need to pull back for a while. If so, let your friend know that you are doing this.

Try not to take rejection personally. Many people who are grieving don't have the energy to be considerate or nice.

Your friendship will probably change throughout your friend's grief. Some friendships deepen, but some drift away. Grieve the loss of the old friendship and be open to changes.

A friendship is deeply affected, even transformed, by grief. Those who have lost a loved one often feel committed to enhancing the quality of their friendships, which can lead to a deepening of some relationships and termination of others. Those who are grieving may demand more of their friends but find, too, that once the most consuming stage of grief is passed, they are able to give more, particularly when called to support friends through a similar life transition.

From the point of view of the friend, while some people may feel catalyzed to support a friend in grief, others may feel overwhelmed by the intensity of that grief and pull away. Thomas Moore reminds us that in either case, the friendship may live on in the imagination: "Eternity makes itself felt in both lasting relationships and those that last only a short time. In neither case is the soul concerned with literal time, but rather with the tone of the event. If it evokes eternity, then the friendship itself remains in imagination for endless time, even if the personal relationship does not" (Moore, p. 97).

In confronting our aloneness and mortality when we lose a loved one, we renew contact with ourselves, discover who we are, and risk a new definition of ourselves. With a clearer sense of self and the willingness to communicate while respecting differences, we can define with new clarity our position in a relationship, one that is based on our own priorities and values. This new congruence of inner and outer realities can enable us to act rather than merely react, thus building the basis for real communication and intimacy in our relationships.

Epilogue

"The end is where we start from," writes T. S. Eliot. When we come to the final pages of a book, we have reached an ending but, if that book has been meaningful to us, the end of a book is also a beginning. As we close the cover, we take within ourselves what has touched and inspired us. Whatever we have read on the page can then become a part of us and of our lives. So it is when a loved one dies. That life is over. Yet, if that person has touched you deeply, he or she becomes a part of you. You will carry that person within yourself always. Many other cultures took this process for granted; nurturing the relationships with the ancestors is an integral part of the fabric of daily life. Deep down, we know this, too, but we have to be reminded.

I hope that this book has challenged any assumptions that have made it difficult for you to connect with a deceased loved one; for example, that death has severed your relationships with loved ones, that it is too late to reconcile, and that you must resign yourself to living with your memories and regrets. I encourage you to let your imagination lead you past these limiting concepts into the unknown, where possibilities beyond your wildest dreams await you. Your imagination is a creative entity, an animating and healing force that can restore to you those you had considered lost.

Imagination heals by stretching you beyond your comfort zone into new experiences. Until her imagination gave her this experience, Kira couldn't conceive of tenderly rocking her father. Until her imagination allowed her to see, Candace considered it impossible to witness her father's life through his eyes. Many of the vignettes Candace witnessed were painful for her to face, particularly the scene in which her father tried unsuccessfully to leave a marriage that was controlled by his mother-in-law. Imagination heals if you can wait for what comes and risk seeing and hearing what it sets before you. As you commit to cultivating and deepening your relationships with deceased loved ones, or with those who are living, for that matter, the internal communication exercises in this book will enable you to express love, work through unresolved issues, and find new possibilities for relating. Take advantage of the freedoms that the imagination provides: to express yourself without restriction, to break out of old patterns of relating, to step inside another person. You may feel exhilarated and excited as you make breakthroughs in old relationship impasses. You may feel immensely grateful to receive or give love that had not been possible when the person was alive. You may also feel vulnerable and raw as you touch old wounds or break through old taboos. Sometimes, to be sure, you may feel discouraged and resistant as you face unpleasant realizations or uncomfortable feelings.

You will experience many of these feelings and pass through several stages as you build a new relationship. First, you must experience the freedom of expressing what you think, feel, and want, including whatever has been repressed, held back, or silenced in your relationship. Amy vented her regrets and resentments in her letter to her deceased father; only then did she feel ready to forgive herself and him. Expressing yourself honestly and authentically to another person in the imagination will help build a sense of self-worth and confidence that is essential in building a healthy relationship.

In the second stage of building a new relationship through writing or speaking a response, you learn to provide a voice to the other person. As you do this, you may feel yourself to be simultaneously within yourself and within the other person, an experience that puts you in touch with that person's feelings and thoughts. This can be even more dramatic when, working with imagery, you step inside another and see the world through his or her eyes. Suddenly, you understand the relationship from the other person's perspective. Compassion, understanding, even forgiveness develop naturally at this stage.

In the third stage, a new relationship has finally emerged. Be prepared for changes in your relationship that didn't seem possible before. As you communicate with your loved one, the dialogue shifts from resolving past issues to an expression of intimacy in the present. After repeated experiences of connecting with your beloved through the imagination, your heart will acknowledge a comforting, affirming presence abiding within—a presence you now trust to be accessible whenever summoned.

But you'll find that this presence incorporates more than you thought: a sense of luminosity, wisdom, and immeasurable peace. You have come face-to-face with a sacred life force that pulses at the center of every being. Through cultivating and deepening your inner relationship with your loved one, you will have touched the divine.

Bibliography

Achterberg, Jeanne. *Imagery in Healing*. Boston: Shambhala, 1985.

Allende, Isabel. *Paula*. New York: HarperCollins, 1994.

Ashley, Judy. "My Mother's Hair" in *Loss of the Ground-Note*, H. Vozenilik, ed. Los Angeles: Clothespin Fever Press, 1992.

Bettelheim, Bruno. *The Uses of Enchantment*. New York: Vintage Books, 1989.

Bradshaw, John. *Bradshaw On: The Family*. Deerfield Beach, Florida: Health Communications, Inc., 1988.

Callanan, Maggie, and Patricia Kelly. *Final Gifts*. New York: Bantam, 1993.

Doore, Gary, ed. *What Survives?*. Los Angeles: Jeremy P. Tarcher, 1990.

Ebbinger, Paul. *Restless Mind, Quiet Thoughts*. Ashland, Oregon: White Cloud Press, 1994.

Eliot, T. S. *Four Quartets*. New York: Harcourt Brace Jovanovich, 1943.

Epel, Naomi. *Writer's Dreaming*. New York: Vintage Books, 1993.

Gray, John. *Men are from Mars, Women are from Venus*. New York: HarperCollins, 1992.

Hijuelos, Oscar. "Oscar Hijuelos, Cuban Author." Interview on "Fresh Air," National Public Radio, 1989.

Hillman, James. *The Dream and the Underworld*. New York: HarperCollins, 1979.

Houston, Jean. *The Search for the Beloved*. Los Angeles: Jeremy P. Tarcher, 1987.

Jung, C. G. *Memories, Dreams, Reflections*. New York: Vintage Books, 1961.

Jung, Carl. "The Spirit Mercurius" in *Alchemical Studies* Vol. 13 of *The Collected Works*, Princeton N.J.: Princeton University Press, 1943.

Kalish, Richard A. and David K. Reynolds. "Phenomenological reality and post-death contact," Journal for Scientific Study of Religion, 1973, 12, p. 218.

Kalish, R. A. and D. K. Reynolds. *Death and Ethnicity*. Los Angeles: University of Southern California Press, 1976.

Kaplan, Louise J. *No Voice Is Ever Wholly Lost*. New York: Simon and Schuster, 1995.

Kennedy, Alexandra. *Losing a Parent*. San Francisco: HarperCollins, 1991.

Kennedy, Alexandra. "Writing Fairy Tales." Mothering Magazine, Spring 1993.

Kramer, Kenneth P. *Death Dreams*. New York: Paulist Press, 1993.

Larsen, Stephen. *The Mythic Imagination*. New York: Bantam, 1990.

Lerner, Harriet. *The Dance of Intimacy*. New York: HarperCollins, 1989.

Levine, Stephen. *Who Dies?* Garden City, New York: Anchor Books, 1982.

McLeod, Beth Witrogen. "The Caregivers" in *The San Francisco Examiner,* April 9, 1995.

Mindell, Arnold. *Coma: Key to Awakening*. Boston: Shambhala, 1989.

Moore, Thomas. *Soul Mates*. New York: HarperCollins, 1994.

Nietzsche, Friedrich. *The Portable Nietzsche*. New York: Viking, 1977.

Nouwen, Henri. *In Memoriam*. Notre Dame, Indiana: Ave Maria Press, 1980.

Roth, Philip. *Patrimony*. New York: Simon and Schuster, 1991.

Saint-Exupery, Antoine de. *The Little Prince*. New York: Reynal & Hitchcock, 1943.

Satir, Virginia. *The New Peoplemaking*. Mountain View, California: Science and Behavior Books, 1988.

Saunders, Dame Cicely. "I Was Sick and You Visited Me" in *Christian Nurse International,* no. 4 (1987).

Savage, Judith. *Mourning Unlived Lives*. Wilmette, Illinois: Chiron Publications, 1989.

Silverbird, Kira. "Losing and Finding My Father," an unpublished manuscript.

van der Post, Laurens. "Dialogues with Sir Laurens van der Post: A Mythic Life." Interview on New Dimensions Radio, tape #2474, December 1994.

Von Franz, Marie-Louise. *On Dreams and Death*. Boston: Shambhala, 1987.

Von Franz, Marie-Louise. *The Way of the Dream*. Boston: Shambhala, 1994.

Walsh, Roger N. *The Spirit of Shamanism*. Los Angeles: Jeremy P. Tarcher, 1990.

Watkins, Mary. *Waking Dreams*. Dallas, Texas: Spring Publications, 1976.